THE EVERYTHING KIDS' Human Body Book

All you need to know about your body systems—
from head to toe!

Sheri Amsel

Adams Media
New York London Toronto Sydney New Delhi

Adams Media
An Imprint of Simon & Schuster, Inc.
57 Littlefield Street
Avon, Massachusetts 02322

An Everything® Series Book.
Everything® and everything.com® are registered trademarks of Simon & Schuster, Inc.

ADAMS MEDIA and colophon are trademarks of Simon and Schuster.

For information about special discounts for bulk purchases, please contact Simon & Schuster Special Sales at 1-866-506-1949 or business@simonandschuster.com.

The Simon & Schuster Speakers Bureau can bring authors to your live event. For more information or to book an event contact the Simon & Schuster Speakers Bureau at 1-866-248-3049 or visit our website at www.simonspeakers.com.

Cover illustrations by Dana Regan
Interior illustrations by Sheri Amsel; page 18 © istockphoto/VladislavMakarov
Puzzles by Beth Blair

Manufactured in the United States of America

Printed by LSC Communications, Harrisonburg, VA, U.S.A.
10 9 8
February 2017

ISBN 978-1-4405-5659-3

Visit the entire Everything® series at *www.everything.com*

CONTENTS

INTRODUCTION

This book is about the most interesting thing on Earth—YOU!

Did you ever wonder how your muscles work or why your heart beats? How many hairs do you have? What are freckles? Why do you get hiccups or sneeze? What are goose bumps? Why do you have a belly button? How do you hear, see, smell, and taste? Why do you shiver when it's cold and sweat when it's hot? These are just a few of the many amazing mysteries about your body that will be explained in this book.

Your body is a machine with a lot of moving parts. It is a very complicated system. There is so much to know that people who work with the human body often specialize in just 1 part of it. A doctor may be a cardiologist and specialize in caring for the heart. A neurologist specializes in the nervous system, including the brain. A dermatologist treats the skin. A podiatrist is a foot expert.

Doctors, nurses, dentists, emergency medical technicians, and biology researchers are just a few of the people who study the human body. An anatomist studies the big parts of the body like the organs, muscles, and bones. A microbiologist studies the tiny, microscopic parts of the body, like the blood, cells, and other tissues. A geneticist studies your DNA. They may help repair injured people or treat sick people or find new ways to prevent illnesses in the first place. They may fix birth defects and extend lives. All these scientists are putting together a pretty complete picture of what is going on inside the human body to help people know the best way to stay healthy and strong for a good, long life. Not everything is known yet, but every day we know more about the amazing human body.

If you are interested in what you read here, maybe you would like to become a doctor, nurse, or other health professional when you grow up!

CHAPTER 1

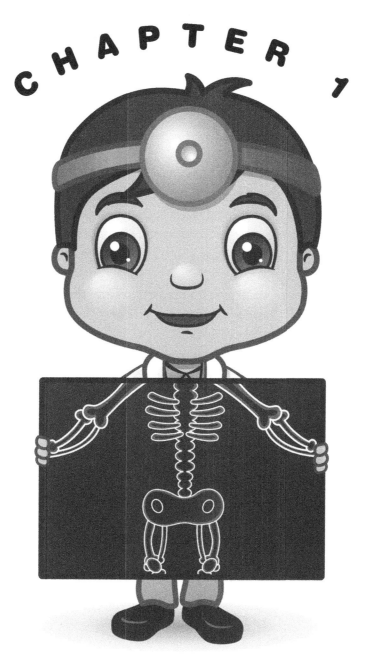

THE AMAZING HUMAN BODY

A Balancing Act—How Does Your Body Work?

The human body is made up of many different systems that work together to form a healthy, functioning person. Without you even knowing it, your body is busily working every second of the day and night to keep you running smoothly. Here are some of the things your body needs to take care of every day.

- You need protection from the outside world against changes in temperature and moisture, bangs and scrapes, and germs and dirt.
- You need a way to make your body move from place to place.
- You need a way to sense what is going on around you so you can respond to it.
- You need to take in food and break it down to fuel your body.
- You need a way to get rid of wastes that your body doesn't need.
- You need to be able to repair yourself when you get injured, grow, and reproduce.

Your body juggles thousands of processes and functions to do these things every day while keeping things stable inside you so you can go about your day. When you think about how complicated the human machine is and how little goes wrong, it is really an amazing feat.

From Head to Toe—Your Body Regions

The body can be broken down into parts and regions, each with its own name. This helps doctors and other medical caregivers know where you might be injured so they can care for you. It helps for you to know what the body regions are called, too.

If you stand at attention with the palms of your hands facing forward and your thumbs pointing out, this is called the *anatomical position*. In this position the terms right and left refer to how you see them, not the doctor looking at you. So your right side is always the side with your right hand. That way, if you complain of pain on the right side of your belly, the doctor knows which

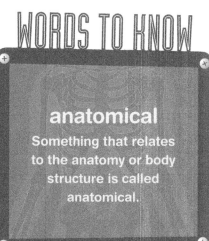

WORDS TO KNOW

anatomical
Something that relates to the anatomy or body structure is called anatomical.

The Body Regions

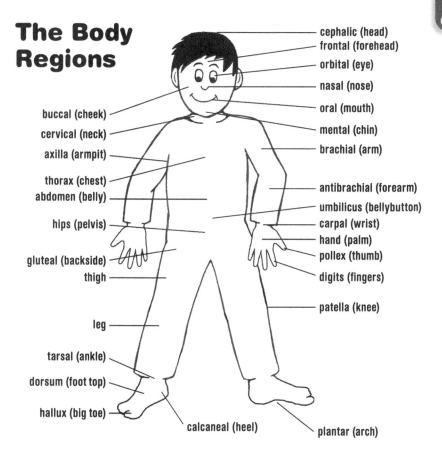

buccal (cheek)
cervical (neck)
axilla (armpit)
thorax (chest)
abdomen (belly)
hips (pelvis)
gluteal (backside)
thigh
leg
tarsal (ankle)
dorsum (foot top)
hallux (big toe)
calcaneal (heel)

cephalic (head)
frontal (forehead)
orbital (eye)
nasal (nose)
oral (mouth)
mental (chin)
brachial (arm)
antibrachial (forearm)
umbilicus (bellybutton)
carpal (wrist)
hand (palm)
pollex (thumb)
digits (fingers)
patella (knee)
plantar (arch)

9

side the pain is actually on! Here are some important terms to remember.

- Your head is *superior* to your shoulders, while your shoulders are *inferior* to your head.
- Your belly button is *anterior* to your backbone, while your backbone is *posterior* to your belly button.
- Your ears are *lateral* to your nose, while your nose is *medial* to your ears.
- Your elbow is *proximal* to your fingertips, while your fingertips are *distal* to your elbow.
- Your skin is *superficial* to your muscles, while your muscles are *deep* to your skin.

You can see how knowing this language could be useful if you are describing where an injury is on someone's body. Suppose someone got a deep cut on his face and needed stitches. Would the doctor know from that description where the cut is? How about if you could describe the cut by saying that it was inferior to the right eye, just lateral to the nose? Can the doctor picture where it is now? Knowing the parts and regions of the body can be a useful healthcare tool.

What's In Your Trunk?

Your trunk is the main part of your body, not including your arms, legs, and head. It is divided into 3 main body cavities, each containing important body organs. They are the *thoracic cavity*, *abdominal cavity*, and *pelvic cavity*.

Health Tip
PROTECT YOUR GUTS!

The body cavity (and its organs) that is most likely to be injured in an accident is the abdominal cavity. That is because, unlike the thoracic cavity that is protected by the ribcage and the pelvic cavity that is protected by the boney pelvis, the abdominal cavity is only surrounded and protected by muscles. This is another good reason to always wear your seatbelt while riding in the car. Protect your guts!

- The **thoracic cavity** is inside your thorax, or chest, and includes your ribcage and the organs inside it—your heart, lungs, and the major blood vessels as they leave and enter the heart.
- The **abdominal cavity** is inside your abdomen, or belly, and includes the organs of your digestive tract—your stomach, intestines, and liver.
- The **pelvic cavity** is inside your pelvis, or hips, and includes the organs inside your boney pelvis—your bladder, reproductive organs, and the end of the large intestine.

Test Your Body Language

Answer the following true or false questions to test your body language.

1. Your shoulder is superior to your knee. — True or False?

2. Your nose is inferior to your mouth. — True or False?

3. Your shoulder is distal to your fingers. — True or False?

4. Your knee is proximal to your toes. — True or False?

5. Your shoulder is lateral to your neck. — True or False?

6. Your ear is medial to your nose. — True or False?

7. Your shoulder muscle is superficial to your shoulder bone. — True or False?

8. Your nose is deep to your skull. — True or False?

(Answers: 1. T, 2. F, 3. F, 4. T, 5. T, 6. F, 7. T, 8. F)

Your Body Parts

It's helpful to know what the parts of your body are really called. You might be surprised when you find out. Here are some official names. Many of the areas are named after the bones that are beneath that spot. See which ones are familiar to you:

- **The head** is broken down into many regions by itself. The forehead is frontal. The nose is nasal. The eye is orbital. The mouth is oral. The cheek is buccal. The top of the head is cephalic. The chin is mental.
- **The neck** is cervical.
- **The arms** have several areas. The armpit is called the axilla. The arm is really only from the shoulder to the elbow. From the elbow to the wrist is the forearm. The wrist is carpal. The hand is made up of the palm (in the front), thumb, and fingers. The thumb is also called the pollex. The fingers are the digits.
- On **the trunk** of your body, the front area is the chest, or thorax. Below that is the belly, or abdomen. Your belly button is the umbilicus. The back consists of the upper back (or dorsum), the lower back (or lumbar region), and the buttocks (or gluteal region). Next come the hips, or pelvis.
- **The lower limbs or legs** have several regions, too. Officially, from the hip to the knee is called the thigh. The kneecap is the patella. Below the knee is the leg. Then comes the ankle or tarsal. The top of the foot is also called the dorsum and the bottom is called the plantar surface or arch, followed by the toes or digits. The big toe is also called the hallux. The heel is called the calcaneal.

START

Head to Toe

Your body is amazing from head to toe, packed full of muscles, nerves, and brains to power you through each day! Use your skill to find the path from START to END.

END

TRY THIS

Moving and Grooving

You can test a lot of body movement while dancing. Put on some fun dancing music and try a few moves with the beat of the music. Flex and extend your arms, legs, and head. Rotate your body at your hips. Rotate one leg and then the other. You're dancing!

You Have a Lot of Good Moves

Body motions have names, too. Some of them are obvious names that you already know. When you bend a joint like your elbow to bring a drink to your mouth, you are flexing your arm. When you straighten the arm again, you are extending. You flex and extend your leg when you walk or run. You flex and extend your head when you nod. You flex and extend your fingers when you make a fist and release it. You flex and extend your body when you bow at the waist.

You do a lot of rotating, too. When you shake your head no, you are actually rotating your head. You can rotate your arms and legs, too. When you turn your palm up, you are rotating your arm laterally (away from your body). When you turn your palm down, you are rotating it medially (toward your body). When you do the twist, you are rotating your body.

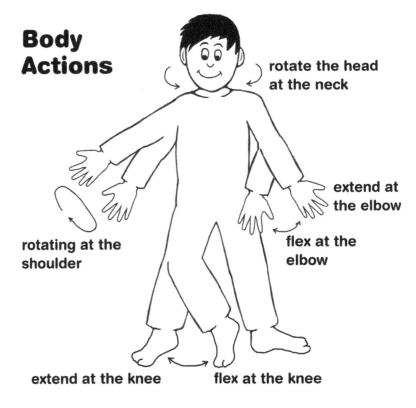

Body Actions

rotate the head at the neck

extend at the elbow

flex at the elbow

rotating at the shoulder

extend at the knee

flex at the knee

The Body's Building Blocks—Cells

Like bricks in a building, your body is made up of cells. Your trillions of cells are working together to keep a balance in the complicated human machine that you are. Like your whole body, each cell grows, adapts, reacts, repairs, uses energy, and reproduces.

Cells are each made up of many important parts:

◆ **Cell membrane:** Cells have a protective outer layer—the cell membrane—that makes sure only the right things go in and out of the cell.

◆ **Cytoplasm:** Inside the cell membrane, many tiny organelles are in a watery medium called cytoplasm. The organelles each have an important job to do to keep the cell—and the body—running well.

◆ **Nucleus:** The nucleus is like the brain of the cell, controlling how things work. The nucleus is also where the DNA is found with all your genetic information.

◆ **Ribosomes:** Other organelles that look like little grains floating around in the cytoplasm are called ribosomes. Ribosomes are where proteins are made.

◆ **Mitochondria:** There are also many mitochondria, the cell power plants. They break down sugar to make ATP, which is used by the cell as energy.

◆ **Lysosomes:** These are the garbage disposals of cells. Little sacs of digestive enzymes, they will take in and break down the things that the cell doesn't need anymore. They also kill bacteria and viruses that invade the body.

These are just a few of the cell's many important organelles.

organelle

Organelles are the "little organs" of a cell that carry out the many jobs that need to be done in a living thing.

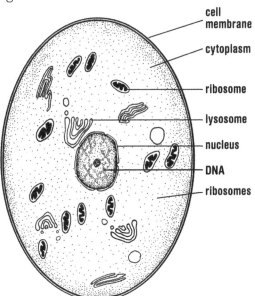

cell membrane
cytoplasm
ribosome
lysosome
nucleus
DNA
ribosomes

The Cell and Its Organelles

Big Cell Breakfast
The cells of the human body are smaller than the eye can see. You would have to look under a microscope to see any of your body cells. However, not all cells are that small. A bird's egg is 1 cell. Have you seen any big cells lately—maybe next to some toast?

You Are a Cell Jigsaw Puzzle
You are made up of up to 100 trillion cells. That's 10,000 billion cells and 1,000,000 million cells. That's a lot of cells.

From Cells to You!
There are many kinds of cells in the human body, each doing its own important job. There are muscle cells, bone cells, and blood cells, just to name a few. Each kind of cell acts a little differently to suit its role in the body. For instance, muscle cells can stretch and snap back into shape to suit the way a muscle needs to be. A nerve cell, on the other hand, doesn't stretch and extend, but already has a very, very long tail down which a signal can be sent from one part of the body to another, as needed by the nervous system.

Groups of like cells together form a tissue. For instance, many muscle cells form muscle tissue. Two or more tissues together form each of our organs, like the heart or lungs. Many organs together form an organ system, like your digestive system. All the organ systems together form an organism, like you! From your smallest part to your whole body, you go from cells to tissues to organs to organ systems to you.

Congratulations! It's a Cell!
Cells don't live forever. Over time they get worn out or injured and die. You need more cells to replace them as you grow up and get bigger. So cells multiply and replace themselves by dividing and making new cells. Cell division is more complicated than you might think. Not only does each cell have to split in half, but all of the DNA inside it has to be copied exactly (replicated) and split in half, too. Scientists break cell division down into many phases to help understand the process. This is called *mitosis*.

Build a Body

Join these jigsaw "cells" together to form a tissue, and then an organ. What are you building? To find out, figure out where each cell goes, and draw the pattern from that piece into the correct space in the empty grid.

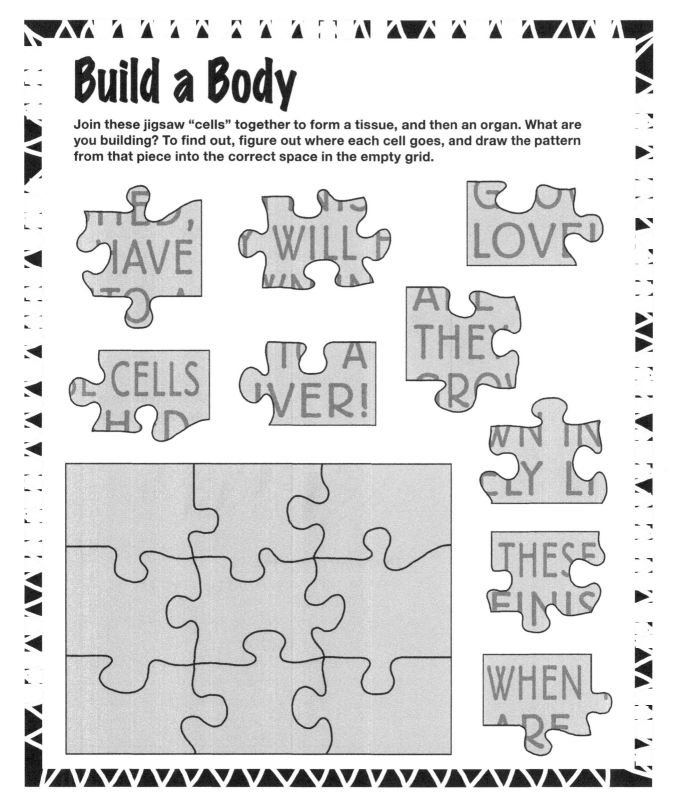

WORDS TO KNOW

chromosome

Chromosomes are butterfly-shaped structures made up of tightly coiled DNA and proteins, found in the nuclei of our cells.

You Are Your DNA

DNA is stored in the nucleus of most of the cells in your body. But what does DNA look like? Physically, your DNA is a very long double-stranded structure that is wound up and coiled into a butterfly-shaped structure called a chromosome. You have 46 chromosomes in each cell's nucleus. Each chromosome carries hundreds (and sometimes thousands) of genes stored on its DNA. Your genes describe some of your body's traits. They describe traits like your hair color, eye color, allergies, body shape, tastes, diseases (like diabetes) you might get, and much more. This is why DNA is called your *genetic code*. It carries the code to build those traits using protein building blocks.

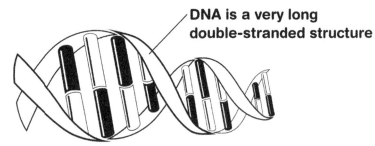

DNA is a very long double-stranded structure

The Power of Protein

There are many reasons why proteins are so important.

◆ Proteins are the building blocks of all living things. They are part of every cell and tissue in the body.
◆ Proteins are used in almost all of the body's functions.
◆ Proteins bring order to what cells do.
◆ Proteins are used for making more DNA and making more proteins. One of the most important things DNA does is to make copies of itself. This is important because as you grow your cells are dividing and making more cells. Every new cell will need an exact, complete copy of DNA.

Are You Man or Mouse?

Considering how complicated a person is, scientists thought that we would have many hundreds of thousands of genes. After the Human Genome Project, where scientists mapped the genes of humans and other species, scientists were stunned to find out that we actually have fewer than 30,000 genes! That is almost the same number of genes as a mouse.

Though we only have about 30,000 genes with code for making proteins, these genes mix and match to come up with more than 120,000 different proteins that the body needs. This is called *alternate splicing* and explains how we can be so complex with so few genes.

When Good Genes Go Bad

A lot of diseases are the result of genes that are not working right. With new understanding of how genes work, scientists have begun to do gene therapy. Some of the amazing things that can now be done to correct bad genes include:

- Scientists can sometimes add a gene into a person's genome to replace a gene that isn't working.
- Scientists can sometimes repair an abnormal gene so that it is working correctly again.
- Scientists can sometimes control when a gene turns on and off to control what it does in the body.

Gene therapy is still in its research phase and is rarely used on humans yet, but good results in tests on animals are very promising.

WORDS TO KNOW

gene

A gene is a unit of heredity that you get from 1 of your parents. Each gene describes 1 or more of your body traits—like eye or hair color—by coding for the proteins that create that trait.

FUN FACTS

Count the Genes

Different species have different numbers of genes. Doesn't it seem like humans would have a lot more genes than any other organism? It turns out that we don't! Here are about how many genes there are in some species you might know:

- ✳ A human has about 30,000 genes
- ✳ A mouse has about 30,000 genes
- ✳ A roundworm has 19,100 genes
- ✳ A fruit fly has 13,600 genes
- ✳ An E. coli bacteria yeast has 3,200 genes

Your Body's Systems

Each body system has many important jobs and works together with other body systems. This keeps the body running smoothly. There are many body systems. Here are a few:

- **The integumentary system** (also called your skin) supports and protects you.
- **The skeletal system** gives you internal support, like the beams in a building, and anchors your muscles so you can move.
- **The muscular system** provides the pull on your bones that allows you to move. Your muscles also warm you up as they work.

Copy Shop

When a strand of DNA makes a copy of itself, it unzips down the middle and adds new protein building blocks to the empty spaces of each half. This makes two exact copies of the original! Can you find the two pieces that will fit each half of this strand?

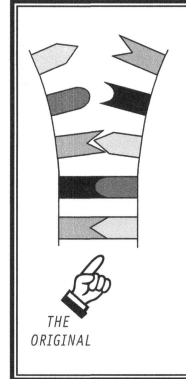

THE ORIGINAL

- **The nervous system** controls all the other body systems. Using electrical impulses to get information and give orders, it is literally the brains of the operation.
- **The endocrine system** makes the hormones that control a lot of your body functions along with the nervous system.
- **The circulatory system** moves food and oxygen around to where you need it and gets rid of waste.
- **The respiratory system** brings you the oxygen you need and takes away the carbon dioxide you don't.
- **The digestive system** breaks down the foods you eat so your body can use it for energy.
- **The reproductive system** is how we make new people!

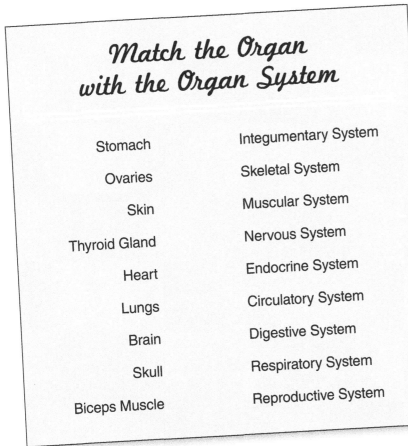

Match the Organ with the Organ System

Stomach	Integumentary System
Ovaries	Skeletal System
Skin	Muscular System
Thyroid Gland	Nervous System
Heart	Endocrine System
Lungs	Circulatory System
Brain	Digestive System
Skull	Respiratory System
Biceps Muscle	Reproductive System

Answers: Stomach–Digestive System | Ovaries–Reproductive System | Skin–Integumentary System | Thyroid Gland–Endocrine System | Heart–Circulatory System | Lungs–Respiratory System | Brain–Nervous System | Skull–Skeletal System | Biceps Muscle–Muscular System

CHAPTER 2

YOUR SKIN IS KEEPING YOU IN

WORDS TO KNOW

integument
The integument is the tough outer layer of an animal that surrounds and encloses it.

blood vessels
Blood vessels are a complex web of hollow tubes that move blood around all through the body. They include arteries, veins, and capillaries.

FUN FACTS

Dead Skin Is Good Skin
The outer layer of the skin, the epidermis, is mostly dead! All but the very deepest layer of the epidermis is made up of dead cells. Even dead, skin cells are important because they protect you from the rough world out there.

Your Skinniest Organ

You probably know that your skin covers your whole body, but did you know that it is actually an organ, like your heart, liver, or kidney? As an organ, your skin has 2 or more layers and a very specific job to do. It is actually the largest organ in the body. It makes up about 7 percent of your body weight. That means that if you weigh 100 pounds, your skin alone weighs 7 pounds! It is also made up of about ½ million cells. Every inch is packed with nerves, sweat glands, blood vessels, and sense organs. These all fit in a layer of skin that, at its thinnest, can be less than ⅟₂₅ of an inch thick (1 mm). There are thicker areas of skin, of course. The places where you rub up against things, like on the bottoms of your feet and the palms of your hands, can be much thicker. Even there, though, the skin is still less than ¼ of an inch (6 mm). Your skin, also known as the *integument*, can be rough in some places like your elbows, knees, and knuckles. It can be very soft and sensitive in some places, like your eyelids and the skin under your arms.

Your Own Body Armor—The Protective Skin Layers

The skin is made up of many layers. The outer layer is called the epidermis. The epidermis is thin but actually has many layers made up of many different kinds of cells. Each has an important job. The outer layer has up to 30 layers of hardened, dead cells. They are rubbed off when you touch things. They act as protection against friction.

One layer of cells makes melanin, a protective coloring (pigment). Melanin protects you from ultraviolet (UV) radiation, the dangerous part of sunlight. Sometimes small patches of melanin pigment will gather together in one place and make a tiny dark spot. This is a freckle! Fair-skinned people usually have more freckles than people with darker skin tone. A lot of sun can give you even more freckles.

Another layer in the epidermis makes keratin cells, which are tough, waterproofing cells. They are formed deep in the skin and then are pushed out toward the surface to help protect you from drying out or getting too wet.

Skin Deep

The inner layer of the skin is the thicker *dermis*, where you find the blood vessels that deliver food, oxygen, and heat around the body. There are also sense organs here, which tell you about how the outside world is affecting you (there will be more about sense organs soon). Hairs are fixed into the dermis, too. So are oil and sweat glands. The oil glands put out oil in a protective film that coats the skin. This helps waterproof the skin and slows down bacteria from growing on the skin. The sweat glands put out sweat that helps cool the skin and keeps you from overheating.

Under the dermis is the *hypodermis*. The hypodermis is mostly a protective layer of fat. It connects the skin to the body like Velcro. About half of all your body's fat is found in the hypodermis!

Your Unique Fingerprints

We all have fingerprints, made by patterns of friction ridges on our finger pads and even toe pads. Though they can be similar, no 2 people have the same fingerprints. Their job is to help you grip things without slipping, but they are more famous for catching criminals.

FUN FACTS

Hungry Cells
Some cells called macrophage cells eat bacteria and other unwanted things that try to invade your skin.

WORDS TO KNOW

melanin
The pigment or protective coloring that keeps us safe from the ultraviolet (UV) radiation of the sun is called melanin. It's also what makes freckles!

keratin
Tough, waterproof cells called keratin are made deep in the skin and then pushed out toward the surface to help protect us.

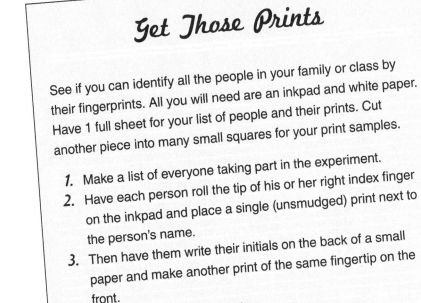

Get Those Prints

See if you can identify all the people in your family or class by their fingerprints. All you will need are an inkpad and white paper. Have 1 full sheet for your list of people and their prints. Cut another piece into many small squares for your print samples.

1. Make a list of everyone taking part in the experiment.
2. Have each person roll the tip of his or her right index finger on the inkpad and place a single (unsmudged) print next to the person's name.
3. Then have them write their initials on the back of a small paper and make another print of the same fingertip on the front.
4. Lay out all the small samples.
5. Match them up with the names on your list.
6. See if you can identify each of the small samples.
7. Check your answers with their initials on the back.

Now you can start your own detective service!

FUN FACTS

Gimme Some Skin

The skin covers your whole body surface. In an adult, that adds up to about 3,000 square inches of skin! That's a lot of skin. A 200-pound adult's skin can weigh up to 14 pounds!

Your Flushing Face

The skin's dermis has many tiny blood vessels, called *capillaries*. They supply the skin with oxygen, food, and heat. In areas of your body that are exposed to cold air, like the head and face, there are more capillaries to give you extra heat. This is a good thing on a cold day when your face is out in the freezing air. But it also means that even a very shallow cut on your face or scalp bleeds a lot more than a cut anywhere else on your body. This is why a cut on your face or scalp seems more serious than in other places—because it bleeds a lot. This is also why your face turns red when you blush!

Skin Art

In each section, use a fine tip black marker to add the given shapes to the thumbprint. In each case you will end up with a familiar picture! Can you guess what each one will be before you complete it?

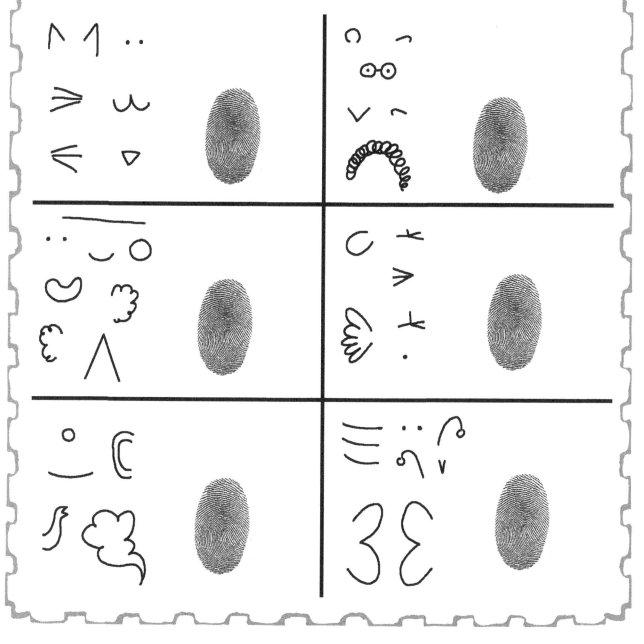

What Your Skin Does for You

Your skin protects you from the outside world, which is always changing. It can be hot or cold outside, wet or dry, sunny or windy. The outside world is also full of bacteria. Some bacteria are dangerous if they get inside you. The many layers of the skin help keep you from feeling the changes outside. It also keeps those bacteria from getting inside your body. This helps keep you in balance, also called *homeostasis*.

The skin is the 1 organ that you can easily see. You look at it a lot! Every morning you look in the mirror and check out this protective organ. How your skin looks can tell you a lot about what is going on inside your body. It gives you clues to many things. If the skin is red and hot, it might mean a fever or an infection. Very pale skin can show shock. A rash can show allergies or infections. Wrinkles show aging. Blisters show injuries from burns, hard work, or even too much sun.

Skin Sensors

There are sense organs in your body that give you information about the outside world. They sense the information (or stimuli) and pass it on to the brain to react to—whether it is smelling, tasting, seeing, hearing, or feeling. The sense organs in the skin are only about feeling. The stimuli you feel in your skin are heat, cold, pressure, touch, and pain. Each of these stimuli are felt by tiny sensors buried somewhere below the surface of your skin. If you get too close to fire, the heat sensors in your skin will let you know it. When someone grips your arm, you feel it with a pressure sensor. If the person squeezes too hard, it alerts a pain sensor. These sensors drive you to act. They remind you to protect yourself. They help keep you safe.

WORDS TO KNOW

homeostasis
Your body adjusting to things happening inside and out is important to keep a healthy balance or homeostasis.

WORDS TO KNOW

stimulus
Something in your environment that stirs you up or pesters you is a stimulus. Your body will respond to a stimulus to protect itself. For example, a bad smell will make you move away!

Your Body Armor

Your skin protects you from the harmful rays of the sun. A sunburn is the first sign that you are getting too much sunlight on your skin. Here is a little experiment to show you how much the sun can damage your skin. The sun is hottest and most dangerous from 11 A.M. to 3 P.M. in the summer, but this experiment will work on any sunny day. Have a grownup remind you of the time, so you don't get an actual sunburn.

1. On a sunny summer day, put on sunscreen as usual everywhere that will be exposed to the sun except the backs of your hands (just for this experiment).
2. Then place a round Band-aid on the back of 1 of your hands.
3. Sit out in the sun with your hands palms down on your knees for about 20 minutes.
4. Leave the Band-aid on and go about the rest of your day (it takes a while sometimes for sun damage to appear on your skin).
5. That night, peel off the Band-aid and compare the backs of your hands.
6. Can you see the round white spot where the Band-aid protected your skin from the sun's rays?
7. Rub sunscreen on your hands to add moisture back into your unprotected skin.

Can you see why sunscreen is so important now?

Health Tip
YOU ARE WHAT YOU EAT

Your skin, like the rest of your body, needs you to eat right to stay healthy. A good diet that includes fruits, vegetables, and lots of water can keep your skin healthy and looking good.

TRY THIS

Right at Your Fingertips

You can test how sensitive different parts of your body are to touch. All you need are 2 small objects that are close in shape and size but not exact, like 2 different house keys or a lemon and a lime. You will need someone to test you.

1. With your eyes closed, have someone roll the lemon on one of your arms (or legs) against your skin and the lime on the other. Can you tell them apart by feeling them with your leg or arm skin?

2. Now handle them with your fingers, rolling them around in your hands. Can you tell which is which now? Can you see how your fingers can feel the differences between the 2, like the size, skin texture, and end bump shapes, where your arm and leg skin cannot?

Where'd You Put That Arm?

There are even skin sensors that let you know where different parts of your body are. This may seem obvious. If you raise your hand to answer a question in class, you know your hand is in the air—but how do you know? Do you look at it? You know it is in the air even with your eyes closed. You sense it. Why is this important? Think about how you step back when the ball comes close to hitting you in a game of dodge ball. Now imagine it is a car, train, or growling dog. It may not always be life threatening. It could be something as simple as not hitting your head on a low doorway or not stumbling on steps, but being able to sense and control where your body is will be important for protecting yourself throughout your entire life.

Making Sense of Things

Because the sense organs receive the information to pass on, they are called *receptors*. All receptors are part of the nervous system. This makes sense, since the messages are traveling to the brain so you can understand them and react. Feeling these stimuli is very important to protect your body. Some are lightning fast. Imagine what would happen if you didn't feel a burning hot pan right away when you picked it up! Some stimuli take time for your brain to react. Have you ever left the house and realized after a bit that you are not dressed warmly enough? It might take a few minutes for the message to spur you into action and go back for a coat.

What Can You Feel?

Some areas of your skin have more receptors than others. Think about which areas may need to have a better sense of feel than others. Can you guess where they might be? If you guessed your fingertips, you are right! You use your hands to feel for things all the time, even when you can't see them. Your fingertips have a lot of receptors, so they are very good at it.

The Touchy Test

You can test your skin receptors with a friend. You will need a glass with ice cubes, a mug of hot water from the tap (never use boiling water), a pencil with an eraser (you will use the eraser end only), and a piece of sandpaper. Ask a grownup to stand by and supervise.

1. Have your friend lay her arm on the table, palm up.
2. Have her close her eyes.
3. Ask her to tell you what she feels. Her choices are touch, pressure, heat, cold, and pain (promise her that you won't make it real pain!).
4. Touch her wrist very gently with the pencil eraser for touch.
5. Press it harder (not hard enough to hurt) for pressure.
6. Touch the bottom of the glass with ice for cold.
7. Touch the bottom of the mug with hot water for heat (press this on your own arm first to make sure it is not too hot to be comfortable).
8. Rub the sandpaper gently for pain—this is meant to mildly irritate, not to really hurt or injure. So be careful!
9. Now let her try it on you.

You have stimulated your skin receptors!

FUN FACTS

Are You Ticklish?
Did you know that when someone tickles you, he is stimulating the touch sensors in your skin? Now if you could just get him to stop!

Hair and Nails Are Skin!

Hair is formed from the skin, but is much less important to you than your actual skin. Hair is mostly for protection, but the amount of hair you have is different from person to person. Some areas on your body have no hair at all, like the palms of your hands or the soles of your feet or your lips. Some places, like your head, are pretty hairy!

Out with the Old

Every minute of every day, old dried up skin cells are flaking off your body and falling all over the place. In fact, most of the "dust" in your house is old cells! Cross out all the words in the grid that either rhyme with old, or have the same meaning as old. When you are finished, read the remaining words from top to bottom and left to right to find out just how many skin cells you shed each day!

GOLD	YOU	ANTIQUE	SCOLD
OUT-DATED	TOLD	AGED	SHED
COLD	TWO	FOLD	TO
THREE	HOLD	BILLION	ELDERLY
ANCIENT	CELLS	MOLD	SOLD
EVERY	SENIOR	DAY	BOLD

Hair has different jobs all over the body. The hair on your head protects you from sunlight and minor bumps and bangs. Humans lose 50 percent of our body heat through our heads, so a good head of hair helps keep us warm, too. Your eyebrows protect your eyes from salty sweat that runs off your forehead. The eyebrow hairs direct the sweat off to the side and away from your eyes. Your eyelashes keep dust and particles from getting into your eyes. Even your nose hairs have a job: keeping particles from getting into your lungs when you inhale.

Is Your Hair Dead or Alive?

Only the hair below the skin is alive. Once it grows out into the outside world above your skin, it is all dead cells, which is why it doesn't hurt when you get a haircut! Hairs don't live very long. An eyelash only lives for about 4 months before dying and falling out to be replaced by a new one. The hair on your head can be there for up to 4 years. We each lose up to 100 hairs off our heads every day.

Scary Hairy

Lots of tiny hairs are rooted in the dermis of your skin. Look at your arms and you can see them. Attached to them are the smallest muscles of the body, called *erector pili*. When your arm hairs are hit by cold air or you have a sudden fright, these tiny muscles will tense (contract) and pull the small hairs upright. This is what gives you goose bumps!

Growing Your Nails

Fingernails and toenails are also formed from the skin. You can pay a lot of attention to your nails as a decoration to your body, but really nails are meant to help you grab and hold onto things. They also protect your fingers and toes, which are both very important to your daily life. Nails grow throughout life.

FUN FACTS

If You Want Your Hair to Grow, Get a Haircut!
The hair on your head grows about ⅓ mm a day. That means its takes about 25 days for your hair to grow an inch. Hair growth also slows down as your hair gets longer. Long hair will go through a resting time where it doesn't grow at all for a while. A haircut will change all that and spur on new hair growth.

Going Bald
People go bald when old hairs die and new ones don't replace them. It is more common in men and is usually inherited, so you can blame it on your ancestors!

Health Tip
WHY YOU HAVE TO WASH YOUR HAIR

Hair is affected by what you eat and your health. Oil glands in the dermis around the base of each hair secrete oil and keep the hair healthy and soft. This is why you have to wash your hair regularly—to clean off the oil that builds up and the dirt and matter that stick to it.

Fingernails only grow about an inch every 6 weeks. Toenails grow even more slowly.

Your nails can reflect your health. The fingernails should look pink in a healthy person. Yellow or split nails can mean a person is not getting enough of the right foods or may be ill. Bluish nails can mean a person is not getting enough oxygen into their tissues. Chewed nails can show a person is under stress. Nails, like the skin, are affected by a good diet and overall health.

Cuts and Scrapes—How Your Skin Heals

Your skin is surrounded by all kinds of dangers every day. It can get scraped, scratched, cut, burned, and bruised. Then it can get swollen, inflamed, and infected. Many injuries are small because the skin is made to be tough for everyday life. But sometimes you do get a serious injury.

Minor scrapes that just affect the outer layer of the epidermis trigger new cells to grow to replace the ones that are scraped off. Injuries that reach down into the dermis or deeper cause a much bigger reaction in the body. If you get a cut that opens up blood vessels in your skin (causing you to bleed), it can cause your heart rate to increase and your body temperature to rise. It also triggers pain and pressure sensors in your skin, so you know you are hurt! A chain reaction begins in your body that will lead to healing (see Chapter 7 to learn about blood clotting).

Sometimes the area where you've had a cut will heal as good as new. Later you won't even be able to tell where the cut was. Sometimes, though, connective tissue fibers will replace some of the skin cells. These fibers look different from the skin around them and will stand out afterward, resulting in what is known as a scar.

Bath Time

Break the Vowel Switch code to find a fascinating fact about your pruney skin! Careful — not all of the words have had their vowels switched.

Q: Why does your skan wranklu when you stoy tee leng in the bothtib?

A: The eitur loyur of duod skan culls soak up wotur. Only parts of it con swull — the rust ef ut is tightly attached to thu skan indurnuoth.

## CHAPTER 3

BONE UP ON YOUR BONES

All about Bones

Your bones keep you upright. Without them you would be like a bowl of Jell-O. They support you like the beams in a building and provide an anchor for all your muscles. This is a huge job because when your muscles work, they need strong bones to pull against, like a lever, to get you moving. Your bones also protect your more sensitive body organs, like your brain tucked safely inside your hard skull and your heart and lungs inside your ribcage.

There are 206 bones of all shapes and sizes in the human body. The largest bone is the femur, or thighbone. It is 2 feet long! It is called a long bone just like all the bones of the arms and legs.

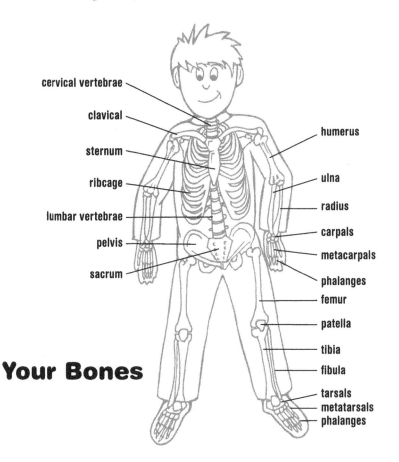

cervical vertebrae

clavical

sternum

ribcage

lumbar vertebrae

pelvis

sacrum

humerus

ulna

radius

carpals

metacarpals

phalanges

femur

patella

tibia

fibula

tarsals

metatarsals

phalanges

Your Bones

These long bones are made to hold up against weight and pressure so you can run, swim, and pick up heavy things. Besides long bones, there are short bones in your wrists and ankles, flat bones like your ribs and skull, and irregular bones like your vertebrae in your backbone. The smallest bone in the body is the tiny staples or stirrup bone in your middle ear. It doesn't do the things the bigger bones do, but helps move sound through the ear so you can hear.

Your Hardy Bones

Bones are so strong because they are made of hard minerals —calcium, phosphorus, and others. These minerals help bones resist rotting, which is why we can still find dinosaur bones even after millions of years! The bones also store the minerals for when the body needs them. If you don't have enough calcium, your body will break down your bones to get what it needs. Bones also store fat inside them for when the body needs it.

Making Blood

Bones are also where new blood cells are made. In the bone marrow, millions of new blood cells are being made every day. This is very important because blood cells only live for a short time and you always need more. To replace all the worn-out red blood cells, the bone marrow can be making as many as 1 million red blood cells every second!

Your Skull Is Full of Holes

The skull is one of the most complex sets of bones in the body. It may seem like one big, hollow bone, but the skull is really made up of 22 bones (not including the jawbone) all linked together. The skull has many important jobs. It must protect your fragile brain. It also protects your eyes and the internal parts of your ears. It

WORDS TO KNOW

vertebrae

The vertebrae are a group of small, irregular-shaped bones that together make up the backbone.

Health Tip

MILK TO THE RESCUE!

Your body needs calcium to grow and repair itself. If you don't eat or drink enough calcium, your body will steal it from your bones! So to keep healthy bones, drink plenty of milk while you are growing.

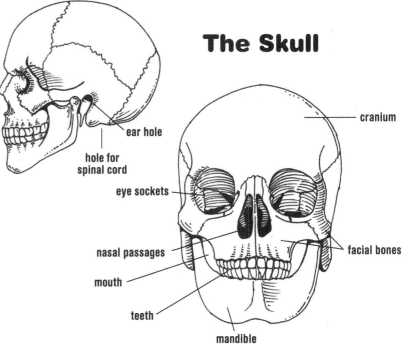

The Skull

cranium

ear hole

hole for
spinal cord

eye sockets

nasal passages

mouth

teeth

facial bones

mandible

Getting Your Head Together
When you are born, the bones of
your skull have not grown together
yet. This is so they can squeeze
together to make your skull smaller
for childbirth and allow your brain
to get bigger as you grow. They
are attached by a tissue sheet and
slowly grow together over your first
2 years of life.

anchors the muscles of your head, face, and neck. The bones in
the front, or your facial bones, are what give you the shape and
look of your face. It is the face you see every morning in the mirror! The facial bones also house the organs for taste and smell.
Together the skull and jawbone, or mandible, hold your teeth and
have the openings through which food and air get inside you.

Holes in Your Head

There are actually many holes in your skull, and each has an
important purpose. There are 2 holes for the optic nerves, which
attach each of your eyes to your brain so that you can see. There
is a hole on each side where sound enters into the ears so you can
hear. There are holes for blood vessels to bring blood to and from
the brain, and holes for nerves to come and go. The very largest
hole is for the spinal cord to pass from the brain down into the
protective vertebrae running down your back.

Say What?

Inside your body are three teeny, tiny bones. They are so small, all three of them together could fit on the fingernail of your pinkie finger! These itty-bitty bones have a very big job to do. When vibrations make them knock together, something amazing happens inside your brain. What is it? Follow the directions to find out!

— **Break the First-to-Last and Number Switch Codes.**

— **Connect the dots numbered 1–16.**

— **Connect the dots lettered A-L.**

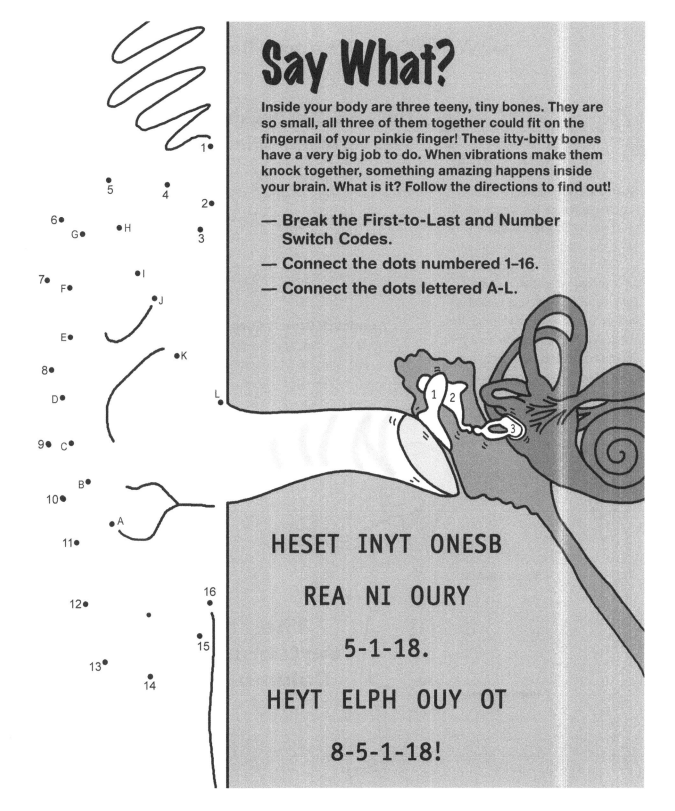

HESET INYT ONESB

REA NI OURY

5-1-18.

HEYT ELPH OUY OT

8-5-1-18!

41

FUN FACTS

Stand Up Straight

Has anyone ever told you to stand up straight? The fact is that the vertebral column isn't straight at all. From the side it has more of an S-shape. This shape gives it a spring-like strength and flexibility that allows us to run and jump. It is still good for your back to hold your shoulders up and your chest out, but it does take energy to hold it that way all day long.

Have a Little Backbone— The Vertebral Column

Your backbone is not really 1 bone at all but many bones, called *vertebrae*. They fit together like the pieces of a jigsaw puzzle. Together these vertebrae make up your vertebral column. The vertebral column stretches from the base of your skull to your hips and is a solid anchor for the powerful muscles that connect the arms and legs to the trunk of your body.

Your Neck Bone's Connected to Your Backbone . . .

There are 7 vertebrae in your neck. They are called cervical vertebrae. There are 12 vertebrae, called thoracic vertebrae, in your upper back that attach to the ribs. The 5 vertebrae in your lower back are called lumbar vertebrae. They are followed by the sacrum and end with the coccyx or tailbone. These bones are held together by very strong fibers, called ligaments, and many muscles. This allows them to work together to keep us upright and walking.

Protecting Your Spine

The bones of your vertebral column each have a hollow ring that together form a long canal. It is through this canal that the spine runs from your brain to your hips. The spine floats in spinal

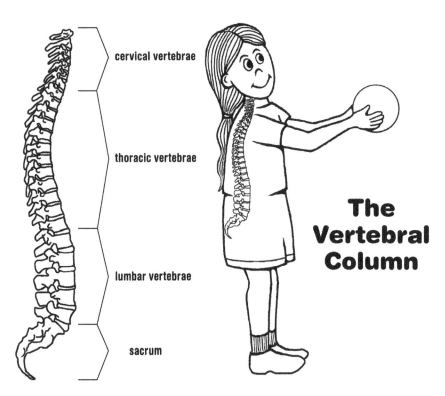

cervical vertebrae

thoracic vertebrae

lumbar vertebrae

sacrum

The Vertebral Column

fluid to protect it from getting banged around when you move. All the nerves bringing messages from the brain to the rest of the body, telling your muscles what to do, come off the spine. (You can read more about nerves in Chapter 5.)

The Body's Shock Absorbers

Between each vertebra are cushion-like pads that soften the shock of our running and jumping around. These pads (or discs) give the back its bounce and stretch (flexibility) when you move. Sometimes a person can hurt a disc in the lower back, often by lifting a very heavy object using only the back muscles. Then the disc may bulge out to the side, pressing on nerves and causing a lot of pain. People call this a *slipped disc* and often need surgery to repair it.

What's Locked in Your Ribcage?

Take a deep breath. Can you feel your chest expand? This is your ribcage, or bony thorax, protecting the heart and lungs inside. Your ribcage is made up of 12 pairs of ribs—24 ribs total. They are held in place in the back by your 12 thoracic vertebrae and in front by your sternum. Your sternum is the flat bone in the center of your chest. You can feel it if you press gently right in the center of your chest between your ribs. Between each rib is a strip of strong muscle that holds them together.

The ribcage is very important. Besides protecting your heart and lungs, it also helps you breathe. When you take a breath, the muscles between your ribs lift and spread your ribs apart. The lungs are attached to the inside of the ribcage, so they get pulled out too, and this pulls air into your lungs like a suction cup.

FUN FACTS

Long-Necked Neighbors
A giraffe has 7 cervical vertebrae in its neck, like you. They are just much longer bones!

WORDS TO KNOW

cervical
Cervical describes things having to do with your neck. The cervical vertebrae are the bones in the neck.

The Incredible Shrinking Grandpa?

You may have noticed that your grandparents are not as tall as they used to be. Are they shrinking? The answer is yes! People do lose height as they age. It's not because their bones get smaller but because the discs between the vertebrae get squashed and flatter over time. They make up about 25 percent of the length of the backbone and can account for as much as 2 inches of height by the time you are your grandparents' age.

WORDS TO KNOW

carpals

The carpals are 8 small bones that make up the base of each of your hands. They sit where the thick, fleshy part of your palm is.

phalanges

The phalanges are the bones in your fingers. There are 14 in each hand—3 per finger and 2 in your thumb.

No Deep Breaths with a Broken Rib

Sometimes you can break a rib in a fall or playing rough sports like hockey or rugby. There is no way to cast a broken rib, but the doctor will often wrap a tight bandage around your chest to help support the ribcage. The problem is that you cannot keep your ribcage still. Every time you take a breath, the ribs expand and separate as you fill your lungs with air. If you have a broken rib, this can hurt! Even just moving around can jolt your ribcage because it is attached to your vertebral column, which bends and moves as you do. People with broken ribs will take small breaths and try not to move around too much for a few days so their ribs can heal. The pain of a broken rib, as with any injury, is a signal for you to take it easy so your body can have time to heal.

Your Arms and Legs

Your arms and legs are pretty useful parts of your body. Your legs allow you to walk, run, and jump, or just stand around waiting in line. Your arms do just about everything you need to do, from eating to turning the pages of this book. It takes a lot of bones working together to make these things happen.

Your arms, including your hands, have 60 bones. Your hands alone have 54 bones. That's a lot of bones moving every time you make a snowball or shuffle a deck of cards. The long bone in your arm (from shoulder to elbow) is called the humerus. The 2 long bones in your forearm (from elbow to wrist) are the radius and ulna. There are 8 small, funny-shaped bones at the base of each hand (16 total for both) called *carpals*. In each of your palms are 5 long, thin metacarpal bones. You can feel them through the back of your hand. There are 14 bones in the fingers of each hand called phalanges. Each of your fingers has 3 phalanges except your thumb, which has 2.

My, What Bony Legs You Have!

Your legs have 60 bones, like your arms. The long bones in your legs are bigger than the long bones in your arms because your legs have to carry your body weight, and that's a lot of work! In fact, the longest bone in your body is the thighbone, or femur. The 2 long bones in your leg (from knee to ankle) are the tibia and fibula. Where the thighbone and the leg bones meet is the knee, and over the knee is the kneecap, or patella. There are 7 small, funny-shaped bones in the heel of each foot (14 total for both), called the tarsals. Over each arch are the 5 long, thin metatarsals. You can feel them through the top of your foot. There are 14 phalanges in the toes of each foot, just like in the fingers.

WORDS TO KNOW

tarsals

The tarsals are the 7 small bones that make up the heel of each of your feet. The 2 largest ones connect to the tibia of the leg.

A Batch of Bones

Match the bones with where they are in your body.

Arm

Leg (calf)

Knee

Forearm

Chest

Foot

Hand

Thigh

Head

Back

skull

vertebral column

femur

patella

ribcage

humerus

tarsals

carpals

radius and ulna

tibia and fibula

Answers: Arm—humerus | Leg (calf)—tibia and fibula | Knee—patella | Forearm—radius and ulna | Chest—ribcage | Foot—tarsals | Hand—carpals | Thigh—femur | Head—skull | Back—vertebral column

Shadow Dance

Skeletons may be made of bones that are hard and unbending, but joints between bones let them move in many marvelous ways! Can you find the group of small skeletons that exactly matches the large dancing skeletons?

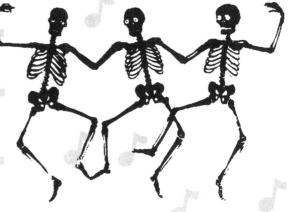

Joints Help You Move

Where 2 bones come together there is always a joint. There are more than 230 joints in your body. We think of joints as a place where a lot of bending and moving takes place. This is true, but joints are also important for keeping your bones tied together. If you bent your knee and your bones flew apart, that wouldn't help you get to school at all! In fact, some joints are bound so tightly that they don't allow any movement at all. An example of this is the joint between your teeth and your jaw. Other than when your baby teeth are replaced by adult teeth, your teeth should never move in their joints. These joints are meant to keep them in place and do—unless you accidentally knock them out (try not to do this!).

Bend at the Knees

Most joints do allow a lot of movement, though not all of them move the same way. There are many kinds of joints in the body that move in many kinds of ways, but in this book we will just look at 2 kinds of joints—hinge joints and the ball-and-socket joints.

Hinge joints only move back and forth, like a hinge. Your elbows, knees, and knuckles are hinge joints. They have limited motion, but they are very stable joints. This makes them good for carrying weight. The next time you lift a heavy rock, notice how powerful and stable your elbows are when only moving in only 1 direction as they do. Your knees are the same way, except they are carrying around your whole body weight on them. So if you fall or are knocked over, your knees are under a lot more pressure. They can be hurt more easily. Luckily, strong muscles and ligaments protect your knees from everyday wear and tear.

Joints

ball & socket joint
• **shoulders**
• **hips**

hinge joint
• **elbows**
• **knees**
• **fingers**

WORDS TO KNOW

ligament

Ligaments are tough bands of connective tissue that hold together 2 bones and help keep joints stable.

Are You Hip to Ball-and-Socket Joints?

Ball-and-socket joints have a full range of motion. This means they allow you to rotate the bones in that joint in a big circle. Your shoulders and hips are ball-and-socket joints. These joints have the most motion of any other joints in the body. This is very useful, allowing you to lift things over your head or hang from your hands. It would be very hard to climb trees or ladders without a ball-and-socket shoulder joint. Unfortunately, because these joints have so much motion, they are not quite as stable as hinge joints.

It is not unusual for people, especially athletes who play rough sports, to pull their shoulder right out of joint. This is called a shoulder dislocation, and it really hurts. In a shoulder dislocation, the top of the arm bone, the humerus, actually gets pulled right out of the shoulder joint. When this happens, that arm becomes useless until a doctor can put the humerus back into place.

Hip joints have less motion, because they are held tightly in place by ligaments and tendons, but they are more stable than shoulder joints. This is a good thing, or you could never climb mountains, ski, or dance!

Sticks and Stones Can Break Your Bones . . .

Even though bones are very strong, they do sometimes get broken. Sometimes you can get a simple break, or fracture, where the bone breaks cleanly under the skin. This can happen in a fall off your bike. The doctor will make sure the bones are set back together and then put on a stiff cast to protect the arm. Over the next 8–12 weeks the bone will heal. Cells will actually lay down new bone at the site of the break and knit it back together over time.

A far worse break is called a compound fracture. This is where the broken bone cuts through the skin. This is much worse because the bone may have a sharp, jagged edge that is harder to heal. It also means there is hurt muscle and skin around the break that must heal, too. These fractures can happen in ski or car accidents. They take a lot longer to heal.

Some broken bones are from sports injuries when the bones are twisted with great force. These breaks are called spiral fractures because of the forceful twist that often makes the break. Though a spiral fracture may not be as bad as a compound break, it can still hurt other tissues, so it takes longer to heal. This can happen playing football or rugby during very rough play.

Word Joints

Look for the body words in the grid. Then look a little further for the second half of a compound word that is hidden at an angle. The first one is done for you.

TOOTH	ARM
HEAD	EYE
LIP	LEG
THUMB	HAND

```
N W O I F T E J L O A D D T
H E A D J O H M T J G E L T
I K T S L D I R Q R G O Y A
M C F O O I R A B O L S K S
E I A R C E P R K O A M C I
G T L L K A P O F M A I I S
T S O O D H O W N D O G P T
H J P I L T R T O O T H J F
U M N E O T D D E R A N I F
M C T E Y E J U M A Z Y S U
B O O M E R A V E R H O W C
J T A C K T Y E L H A N D J
```

Find a Real Skeleton of Your Very Own

You can dissect an owl pellet and find the skeleton of the mouse it ate. This may sound disgusting, but it's really cool. Owls will eat a mouse and spit out the bones and fur into a little pellet. Scientists collect and sterilize them, and you can buy one! Look up owl pellets online or see the websites in the reference section at the end of this book. All you will need is some old newspaper, 3 paper plates, some toothpicks, Elmer's glue, and tweezers (if you have them).

1. Lay out the old newspaper on your kitchen table and then put your 3 paper plates on it.
2. Put your owl pellet on 1 of the paper plates. Open the tinfoil and carefully pull the pellet out onto the plate.
3. Use toothpicks to pick it apart. You will see some white bones. Pull them out and clean them off. You can use your fingers as long as you wash your hands with soap afterward. Remember, these pellets are sterilized.
4. Lay the clean bones on a clean paper plate.
5. When all the bones are out and cleaned off, throw out the paper plate with the debris on it.
6. Now use the picture of the mouse skeleton (one should come in the kit or you can find one online) to identify all your bones. You can lay them out so they are in the right place for a skeleton.
7. Glue the bones 1 at a time to the third paper plate using the Elmer's glue. Put it somewhere safe to dry.
8. When it is dry you can write the names next to each bone on the plate. You have your first animal bone collection!

Here's Looking Through You!

The doctor can tell how badly a bone is broken by taking an X-ray. An X-ray has more energy than light, and when shined on the body, actually goes through it. It doesn't get through all your tissues though, mostly just the soft tissues. It can't get all the way through your dense bones. This is very helpful for looking at your bones. The doctor puts film behind your injured bone and shines the X-ray at it. The X-ray shines through you to expose the film, taking a picture of the bone and any breaks quite clearly. What a useful tool! X-rays are powerful, though, and can be dangerous because they use radiation. That is why the doctor uses a very low dose of X-ray and protects you with a lead apron so only the area needing to be seen is exposed to the radiation.

Old Bones

As people age, sometimes their bones can get fragile and weak. This is called osteoporosis. In some elderly people with osteoporosis, their bones can break on their own without falling or getting any injury at all. You can imagine how scary that might be. In general, most people have a broken bone or two throughout their lives. If you have a good diet, any broken bone should heal just fine. Just be careful not to get too many!

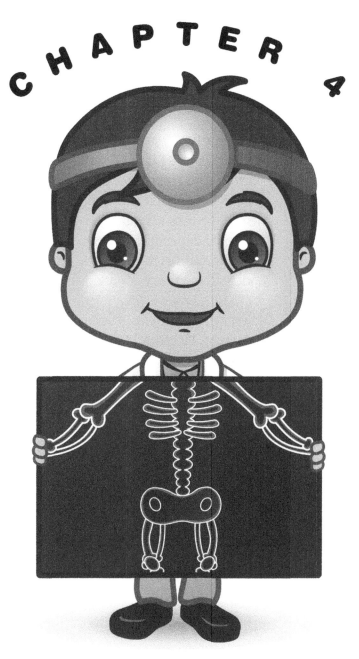

## CHAPTER 4

MUSCLE YOUR WAY THROUGH LIFE

WORDS TO KNOW

contract
When a muscle becomes shorter and more compact in order to move part of the body, it has contracted.

FUN FACTS

Shiver Me Timbers
If your body gets very chilled, it will automatically try to get some heat going by making your skeletal muscles move on their own. This is the reason for shivering and means you need to get somewhere warm soon!

What Is a Muscle?

Muscles are the machines that work the body. All muscles are made up of fibers that allow them to squeeze down small—contract—and then stretch out long again—relax. Your muscles contracting and relaxing is what allows you to move. When you turned the page just now, the muscles in your arms contracted and relaxed to make it happen.

Your muscles help you stay upright all day long. You might not notice it, but gravity is working on you all the time, pushing you toward the ground. After a long day, when your muscles are tired, you might collapse on the couch and lay your head back. Gravity is winning. By bedtime you'll be flat on your bed and let your muscles recover their strength for a few hours while you sleep.

Muscles even keep you warm. Ever notice what happens after you run a race? Your body sweats. You take off your sweatshirt. You fan your face. That is because your big muscles give off heat when they work.

How Muscles Work

Muscles have some really amazing abilities. We know they get us moving, keep us upright, protect our joints, and keep us warm, but how do they do it? Muscles have special traits that allow them to do these helpful tasks for us.

◆ **Muscles are excitable.** That means that they can get messages from your brain and body and get excited by them—they respond to them.
◆ **Muscles are contractible.** That means that they can change shape when you tense them, going from long and thin to short and thick with a lot of force. They contract and they do this in an instant.

- **Muscles are extendible** so you can stretch and extend them when you relax them.
- Most importantly, **muscles are elastic**. This means that they can change shape back and forth over and over again, always recoiling back into shape every time after being stretched.

How do muscles go from long and thin to short and thick? Every muscle in your body is made up of hundreds of thousands of tiny muscle fibers. When a muscle contracts, all the tiny fibers slide by each other, forming a shorter but much thicker bulk, like sliding 2 piles of playing cards together.

The Muscles You Tell to Move— The Voluntary Muscles

There are 3 types of muscles in the body—skeletal muscle, smooth muscle, and cardiac muscle.

Skeletal muscle makes up almost half of the bulk of your body. If you squeeze your thigh, calf, or arm, you are squeezing skeletal muscle. These are the muscles that move your arms and legs along as you swim, run, or climb. Skeletal muscles are sometimes called *voluntary muscles*. That is because you are in control of them. You decide to walk over and turn off the television or pet the dog. You smile at a friend or throw a snowball. You lick an ice cream cone or chase a butterfly. Your brain told those muscles to get moving.

When you want to move, a signal goes from your brain to the skeletal muscles of your legs or arms, like a bolt of electricity. The muscles contract quickly and powerfully. This pulls on the bone to which they are attached and it makes you move!

TRY THIS

Feel Those Muscles

Have you ever seen a bodybuilder flex his muscles by bending his arms at the elbows so his biceps muscle gets bigger? What you are seeing is all the muscle fibers sliding together to make a shorter, more compact muscle. Ask a muscular person you know, like your dad, to flex his arm muscles. Feel the muscle. Even though it is the same muscle, it is much harder and thicker when it is flexed than when it is relaxed.

Health Tip

FEED THE MACHINE

Have you ever gotten a terrible cramp in your leg during a long game of soccer? It hurts and feels like your muscle is all bunched up—like it's stuck contracting and won't relax. The truth is that is exactly what a cramp is. Your skeletal muscles need energy and minerals like calcium and potassium to contract and relax during exercise. If you are sweating out all your minerals and using up all your energy, sometimes your muscles will get stuck in a contraction. Take a break and drink a mineral drink or have a snack.

Pull and Pull

Muscles work in pairs — one pulls in one direction, while the other pulls in the opposite direction! Which six pairs of opposite words can you use to describe these two people?

1._____

2._____

3._____

4._____

5._____

6._____

1._____ 4._____

2._____ 5._____

3._____ 6._____

Tendons Tend Your Muscles and Bones

Because skeletal muscles use a lot of force, they are protected and made stronger by tough connective tissue coverings. They look a little like they are shrink-wrapped. These then attach to tendons that attach the muscles to the bones. One muscle may have a few tendons that attach it to several bones at a time. An example of this is the forearm muscles that flex and extend the fingers. One muscle, called *extensor digitorum*, is attached to your pointer, middle, and ring fingers. When it contracts, it works with other muscles to open your hand.

WORDS TO KNOW

tendon

A tendon is a strong cord of fiber that attaches a muscle to a bone.

Skeletal Muscles

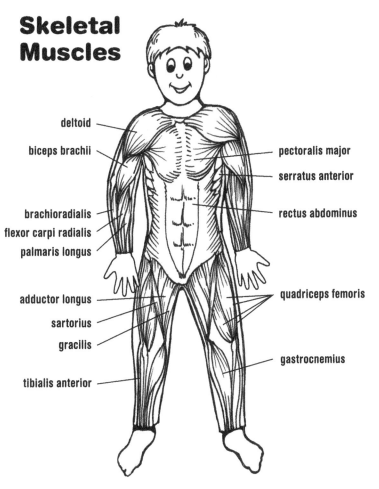

- deltoid
- biceps brachii
- brachioradialis
- flexor carpi radialis
- palmaris longus
- adductor longus
- sartorius
- gracilis
- tibialis anterior
- pectoralis major
- serratus anterior
- rectus abdominus
- quadriceps femoris
- gastrocnemius

TRY THIS

Funky Fingers

Your fingers are flexed and extended by the muscles in your forearm. Some fingers have more muscles helping them than others. Your pointer has a lot of muscles working it, which is why you use it a lot. The finger that has the least help is the ring finger, and it is tightly bound to the workings of the middle finger. You can test this. Lay your hand flat on the table. Now lift each finger, 1 at a time, as high off the table as you can, holding down the others. You won't have any trouble lifting your thumb, pointer, middle finger, or pinky by themselves, but the ring finger will not lift as high without the help of its neighbors.

Muscles Working in Pairs

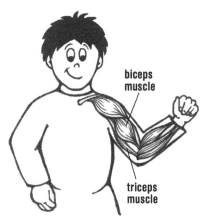

biceps
muscle

triceps
muscle

Muscle Pairs

Skeletal muscles work in pairs. That's because for every action there are usually 2 motions. Think about that. When you turn a book page you reach or extend your arm at the elbow to grab the page. That uses 1 muscle group. Then while turning the page you pull your arm in, flexing at the elbow. This uses the opposite muscle group. This seems like a lot of thought and effort, but in real life it takes just a second to do it.

Moving Is a Group Effort

Skeletal muscles that bend joints work in pairs. You can feel them each at work when you flex your elbow. Try it.

1. Use your left hand and grab your right arm around the widest part between the shoulder and elbow. Have your fingers around the top and your thumb around the bottom. Don't hold on too tight, just firm enough to feel the muscles in your right arm under your fingers of your left hand.
2. Hold your right arm out straight. Now make a fist with your right hand and bend your arm at the elbow slowly.
3. Then straighten your arm again.
4. Do this several times slowly.
5. When you bend at the elbow you are using your biceps muscle under your fingers. Can you feel it shorten and bunch up as it contracts? Try it again with your fist clenched tighter.
6. When you straighten or extend your arm, you are using the triceps muscle under your thumb. Can you feel it shorten and bunch up as it contracts?
7. You can try the same activity flexing your foot and holding your calf muscles. They really are working in pairs!

FUN FACTS

Use It or Lose It

Muscles have to be used to stay healthy. If someone is bedridden from illness, the muscles begin to break down almost right away. You can lose as much as 5 percent of your muscle power for every day you lie around in bed not moving. So it would take less than a week of lying on the couch to lose much of your fitness. Being a couch potato can be bad for your health!

Frown or Smile?

This saying has been around for more than 70 years, "It takes 50 muscles to frown, but only 13 to smile. So smile — it's easier!" Is this saying true? Deciding which of the 53 muscles in your face are used to smile or frown is almost impossible. Let's just say it's more fun to smile!

Draw the correct expression on each empty face. Then make a path that alternates a FROWN with a SMILE, ending with a SMILE. If your path comes to a face that has a STARE, or a WINK, you are going the wrong way!

smile   frown

wink   stare

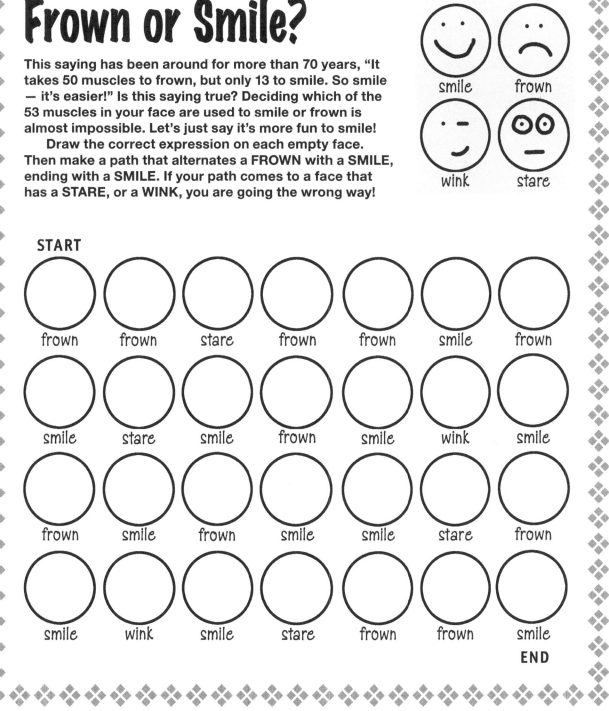

START

frown	frown	stare	frown	frown	smile	frown
smile	stare	smile	frown	smile	wink	smile
frown	smile	frown	smile	smile	stare	frown
smile	wink	smile	stare	frown	frown	smile

END

diaphragm

The diaphragm is a dome-shaped layer of muscle that separates the chest from the belly. The lungs sit on top of it and are attached to it. The diaphragm pulls down when you inhale, pulling the lungs down with it. This opens them up like a suction cup, drawing oxygen into the lungs. In this way, the diaphragm helps you with your breathing.

TRY THIS

Smooth Muscles Working Smoothly

Take a deep breath. Can you feel your chest expand? Your lungs are expanding when you inhale, and then recoil back into shape when you exhale. They can do this because they are lined with smooth muscle. They do it without you having to think about breathing.

The Muscles You Don't Think About— The Involuntary Muscles

The muscles you have little or no control over are called the *involuntary muscles*. Both the smooth muscles and the cardiac muscles of the heart are involuntary muscles. These muscles are told what to do by signals from the brain and body sent out without you even knowing it.

The smooth muscles are spread out all over the body doing important jobs while you are busy doing other things. They contract and relax like skeletal muscles but more slowly, so they can work for a long time without getting tired. Smooth muscles line the walls of all your organs like the stomach, lungs, bladder, and diaphragm. These smooth muscles are spread out in sheets, but are still connected so they can contract together like a team. They are important for organs that expand and contract when they are working. Think how much your stomach muscles work during Thanksgiving dinner!

Smooth Muscles Help Blood Flow

Smooth muscle lines all your blood vessels as well. The blood vessels are the arteries and veins that carry your blood around. This is a really important job, because when you are exercising your body needs more oxygen. That's why you breathe hard. The blood delivers that oxygen to the skeletal muscles that need it. The smooth muscles lining your blood vessels allow them to expand for the surge of blood you need and contract again afterward. You don't have to tell your body to do this. It is involuntary, but you can feel it by the pounding of your heart.

Your Heart Is a Muscle

The other involuntary muscles are the muscles of the heart—the cardiac muscle. Most of the heart is made up of muscle. Cardiac muscle is like skeletal muscle—when it contracts, it contracts fast and hard, and then relaxes. But cardiac muscle, like smooth muscle, works without you knowing. It has to keep your blood pumping night and day, even while you are asleep. All the muscle in the heart is linked so that it will contract in a wave to keep the blood moving through it. With every heartbeat, a muscle contraction sends blood on its way to feed the body what it needs.

Your Face Muscles

Some of the most important skeletal muscles are not the biggest ones. They are the muscles of the face. There are 2 kinds of face muscles. There are the face muscles that help you smile and frown, called the muscles of facial expression. Then there are the chewing muscles, called the muscles of mastication, that help you eat.

Your chewing muscles open and close your jaw so you can mash food between your teeth to make it small enough to swallow. They include your cheek muscles, which help keep food in between your teeth for good chewing action. These are powerful muscles and without them you would probably starve. The tongue is an important muscle, too. It helps you mash and mix food and then it helps you swallow it. It is the tongue that forms your words when you talk, too. Just think how hard it would be to talk with no tongue!

WORDS TO KNOW

mastication
The act of chewing your food is called mastication.

Making Faces

The muscles of the face have many jobs. Most are paired with another one on each side of the face. Sometimes many facial muscles help with each job. There are muscles for blinking, smiling, frowning, flaring the nostrils, furrowing the brow, raising an eyebrow, pouting, grimacing, laughing, and even for kissing! Not all animals have these muscles. Your dog may be able to bare its teeth and blink its eyes but it cannot wink, grin, purse its lips, or frown.

Facial muscles are really important in human communication. You can tell how people are feeling just by how they use their

WORDS TO KNOW

palsy

A palsy is when some muscles become frozen in place (paralyzed) and sometimes have shaky tremors.

TRY THIS

Eye Exercise

You can try out your eye muscles. Put your elbows on the table. Rest your chin in your hands to keep your head from turning. Now try to see as far to the right and left as you can without turning your head. Now try to see as far up and down as you can without moving your head. That is the range of motion of your eye muscles. Don't work them too long though, because they get tired fast! Close your eyes afterward and rest them for a minute.

Play the "How Am I Feeling" Game

You can use the muscles of facial expression to let people know how you are feeling. Try this game to see how it works.

1. On small pieces of paper write the following feelings. Write only 1 on each paper. Write: happy, sad, scared, mad, bored, sleepy, angry, laughing, crying, fierce, secretive, surprised, and embarrassed.
2. Fold each paper up and drop them all in a bowl and mix them around.
3. Have all your friends choose a paper and make a face for everyone to see.
4. Everyone should guess what feeling they are showing with their facial muscles.

You may not guess all of them. Some feelings are more complex and hard to express with just a face, but you can see from this activity how important the muscles of facial expression are to communication.

facial muscles. Someone can show happiness or sadness, and can also use these muscles to scare someone off or welcome someone in. They are very powerful muscles, but not because they are big and strong.

Losing Face

The facial nerve controls the muscles of facial expression on both sides. Sometimes the nerve gets inflamed on one side and a person can lose control of all the muscles on that side of the face. This is called Bell's palsy. It is a strange and upsetting problem because that whole side of the face will droop. If you smile, only the working side will smile. The palsy side will hang lax. The eyelid will droop. Even the tongue will lose taste on that side!

The Eyes Have It

Each of your eyes needs its own set of muscles. They are small, strap-like muscles that allow you to move your eyes back and forth without moving your head. They also allow you to keep your eyes on an object even though you are moving your head. They are some of the fastest-moving skeletal (voluntary) muscles in your body. They respond quickly when you need them. This helps protect you from dangers in the outside world that you need to avoid. Have you ever caught sight of something just in time to duck? You can thank your fast-moving muscles!

Health Tip

SEEING DOUBLE

When the muscles of the eye are not lined up, a person can have trouble focusing her eyes. This is called double vision. This can be treated with eye exercises to strengthen the weaker muscles. If it is bad enough, it can be treated with eye surgery.

Can't Stop!

Now and then, one of your muscles goes out of control. It gets irritated, and starts to spasm, and squeezes in and out like crazy! It drags air into your lungs so fast that a flap of skin inside your throat bounces your vocal cords and produces a very distinct sound. What the heck is going on? Color in all the squares with a vertical line to find out!

The Tiny Muscles

There are some muscles that are even smaller than those of the face. Some are downright teensy-weensy. The smallest skeletal muscles are in the middle ear. They attach to 2 of the tiny ear bones—the malleus (hammer) and stapes (stirrup). When you hear a sound, these muscles contract, pulling the bones apart to protect the inner ear from too much vibration. The louder the noise, the harder they contract. At a loud music concert, these muscles get a real workout. They are 2 of the few skeletal muscles that are not under your control.

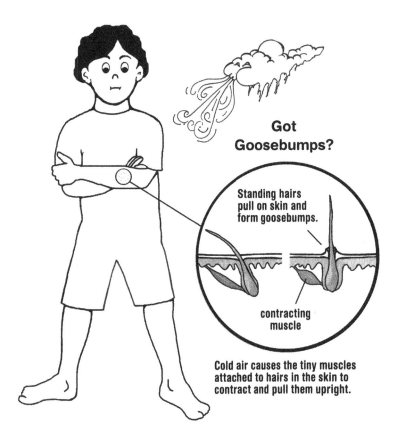

Got Goosebumps?

Standing hairs pull on skin and form goosebumps.

contracting muscle

Cold air causes the tiny muscles attached to hairs in the skin to contract and pull them upright.

Standing on End

Another tiny muscle is found in the skin, attached to each of the tiny hairs found there. They are called the erector pili muscles. Their name means "the one that makes the hair stand up." Their name fits their job! When you get a chill from cool air or a fright, the tiny muscles contract and make the little hairs stand up straight. When the hairs pop up, they pull on the skin. This forms goose bumps.

They are smooth muscles, so they react without you knowing it. The next time you are out in the cold and get goose bumps, you will know your tiny muscles are working.

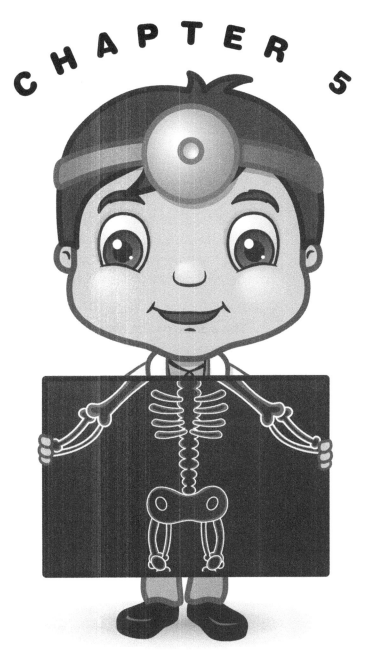

## CHAPTER 5

YOU'VE GOT SOME NERVE!— THE NERVOUS SYSTEM

FUN FACTS

Electric Dinner Bell
Some animals can actually pick up the electrical signals that the nervous system and muscles are making. This is called *electroreception* and is one way that sharks find prey in the ocean. They detect the slight electrical impulses of swimming fish and people! So it's not just the movement that catches their eye. It's the electrical signal that calls them to dinner.

WORDS TO KNOW

integration
Integration is when you bring things together to make a larger and more complex whole to solve a problem. In the nervous system, the information (or stimulus) is brought into the brain so the brain can decide how to react to it.

A Job That Takes Nerve

The nervous system controls the workings of your body with a huge communication network. It keeps track of everything going on to keep your body running smoothly and in balance. The nervous system is fast. It sends messages as fast as lightning. As a matter of fact, like lightning, the messages are electrical signals. If you could see all the electrical signals shooting through your body all the time, you would be surprised at all the fireworks. The nervous system is busy working even when you are asleep.

The 3 Jobs of the Nervous System

The nervous system has 3 main jobs:

1. First it gets information, or stimulus, from the outside world and brings it in. The millions of nerve cells that sense the stimulus are called *sensory receptors*. The stimulus is called *sensory input*. If you wake up in the morning and see the light shining in the window, smell bacon cooking, and hear your mother calling that breakfast is ready, you have gotten 3 kinds of sensory input. Those are just the 3 stimuli you might notice right off, but the truth is, your brain is getting sensory input from all kinds of body sensors all the time. You know if you are hot, cold, hungry, thirsty, sleepy, sore, itchy, lying down, standing up, falling, or stung by a bee, because your brain gets the stimulus and tells you what it is.

2. The second thing the nervous system does is to decide what to do with all that sensory input. This is called *integration*, because it integrates, or unites, the stimulus with what you are going to do about it. Your brain puts together morning, yummy bacon, and mom's calling, and tells you—get up and get dressed!

3. The third thing that the nervous system does is it triggers action. This is called *motor response* or *motor output*. Your muscles respond to orders. You jump out of bed, get dressed, and run down for breakfast. You can think of it like the motor of a car making the car move. Motor means action!

What Is a Nerve?

Messages to and from the brain are carried by nerve cells. Nerve cells (or neurons) are made for carrying nerve impulses—like an electrical wire carrying an electrical signal. Nerve cells have a body that receives the information. They also have a very, very long tail called an *axon* that carries the message to its destination. These axons are smaller than the tiniest thread but travel together all over the body grouped together in bundles called nerves. You have thousands of nerves running signals all over your body all the time. The nerves then branch smaller and smaller to pick up and drop off their messages to every muscle and every inch of skin in your body.

The Nerve Cell

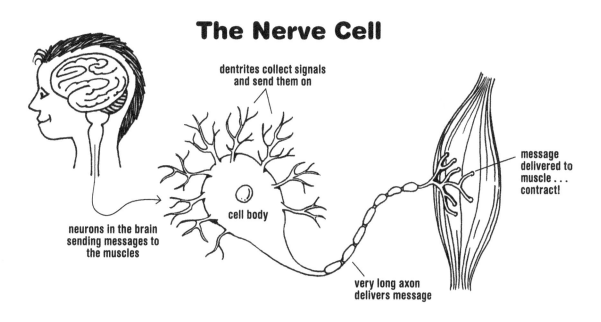

dentrites collect signals and send them on

cell body

neurons in the brain sending messages to the muscles

very long axon delivers message

message delivered to muscle ... contract!

Every nerve is like a message superhighway with many, many, many lanes. Each lane is 1 nerve cell axon carrying messages at high speed. There are millions of nerve cells working all the time and bundled together as nerves. They branch off and exit when they reach their destination. The message is delivered through tiny finger-like projections, called *dendrites*, to the muscle or gland.

Bridging the Gap

Sometimes a message has to go so far in the body that it takes 2 nerve cells to get it there. The first nerve cell will pass the message on through its dendrites to the next nerve cell. Then that nerve cell sends the message down its long axon to its final destination. The tiny space between 2 nerve cells, or the nerve cells and their target muscle, is called a *synapse*. Like water running down a hose to shoot out the end though a sprinkler head, the message reaches the end of the axon, flows into the many branches of a dendrite, and then must cross the gap of the synapse to reach the other side. But instead of the electrical signal leaping across the space, a chemical message flows out and across the synapse to the target muscle or gland. This happens very fast.

TRY THIS

Speedy Messages

You can test how fast your brain gets a job done. Remember, your brain has to get the stimulus, integrate the information, and send out the motor response. Are you ready? Here goes. As quickly as you can, put down this book and clap your hands. How long did it take?

The Nerves That Run the Show

The nervous system is made up of the brain, the spinal cord, and all the nerves that come off your brain and spinal cord. Even though all these parts work as 1 unit, scientists break your nervous system down into 2 systems—the central nervous system and the peripheral nervous system.

The *central nervous system* includes just your brain and spinal cord. Remember that the spinal cord runs down your back inside that canal of protective bone made by the vertebral column. The

Yum or Gross

To some people, broccoli is a vegetable that tastes OK. But to other people it is the most disgusting, horrible, gross, and nasty taste on the face of the Earth! What's going on? While most people have about 10,000 taste buds in their mouth, others have twice that number. These people are especially sensitive to things that taste bitter — like broccoli.

Figure out the Fraction Code to learn the special name that "taste researchers" have given to these picky eaters.

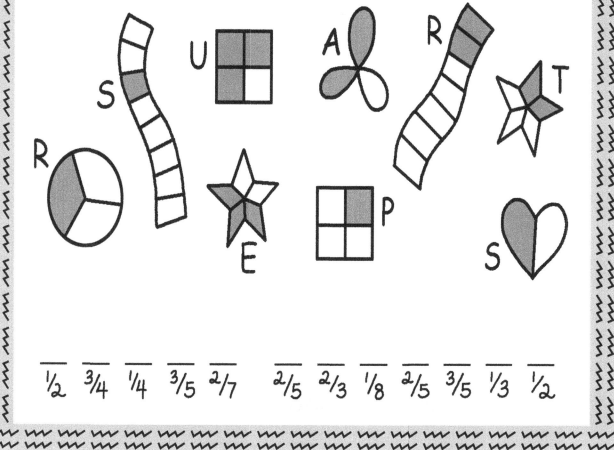

$\overline{}$ $\overline{}$ $\overline{}$ $\overline{}$ $\overline{}$ $\quad$ $\overline{}$ $\overline{}$ $\overline{}$ $\overline{}$ $\overline{}$ $\overline{}$ $\overline{}$

½ ¾ ¼ ³/₅ ²/₇ ²/₅ ²/₃ ⅛ ²/₅ ³/₅ ⅓ ½

central nervous system is the command center of the body. It gets the information, decides what to do with it, and gives orders. The *peripheral nervous system* is everything outside the cerebral nervous system. This includes all the nerves coming off the spinal cord and brain—the spinal nerves and cranial nerves.

Who's the Brains of This Operation?

Looking at the brain, it's hard to believe that it is so important to your life and that it controls everything you do, say, or think. The average brain weighs less than 4 pounds and is soft, pink, and wrinkled like a walnut or a strange coral reef animal.

The brain has 3 major parts—the cerebrum, the cerebellum, and the brain stem. The brain has been described as being shaped like a mushroom, with the brain stem as the stalk and the cerebrum as the cap of the mushroom drooping down and closing over the top of the stalk. The cerebellum sits in back, inside and under the cap.

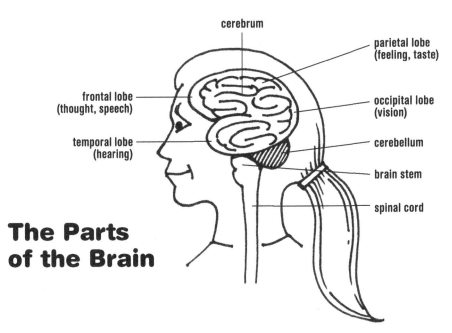

cerebrum

parietal lobe
(feeling, taste)

frontal lobe
(thought, speech)

occipital lobe
(vision)

temporal lobe
(hearing)

cerebellum

brain stem

spinal cord

The Parts of the Brain

The cerebrum is the largest part of the brain, making up about 85 percent of it. It has 2 matching sides, or hemispheres, connected in the middle. It looks a bit like the inside of a walnut, if you could get it out of the shell whole. Like a walnut, it is also covered with twisting ridges and grooves.

The Cerebrum

The cerebrum is broken down into several lobes that have many different jobs:

- The front part of the brain is called the **frontal lobe**. That is where a lot of your thoughts come from. You understand these words and think about them in your frontal lobe. The speech center is in the frontal lobe. Your ability to make your body move is also found here.
- The sides are called the **temporal lobes**. That is where you process and understand the things you hear. If you hear a fire alarm you don't just hear it, you understand what it means.
- The lobe in the very back is called the **occipital lobe**. That is where your vision center is located. That is why if you fall and hit the back of your head you can see bright lights (seeing stars). You have bonked your vision center!
- The upper back half is the **parietal lobe**. This is the big sensory location. You feel everything from a toothache to a stubbed toe here.

What Is Gray Matter?

The cerebrum is different on the outside than it is on the inside. It has an outer layer, like the bark of a tree, that is called the *cerebral cortex* and is gray in color. People sometimes call this their gray matter. The gray matter is where all the nerve cell bodies are found, so it is like the brain of the brain!

The inner part of the cerebrum is mostly white. This is where all the nerve cell axons run from their cell bodies (in the gray matter) down through the spinal cord on their way to other parts of the body.

The gray matter of your cerebrum is where your personality lives. This part of your brain lets you talk, listen, and understand what people say to you. It lets you remember what happened this morning and last year. It is where you feel the things around you like heat, cold, smells, and sights, and understand what they are. It also allows your body to respond to them.

Here is an example of how you might use your gray matter. If you suddenly realized that you smelled smoke, you might wonder for a few seconds what it was, but then you would understand and spring into action. You would jump up to see where it was coming from. If there was a fire, you would decide if it was small enough to put out or if you should just escape and call for help. These thoughts and decisions use your memory about what you have learned about fire, your judgment about how bad the fire is, and your problem-solving skills about what to do. They are a very complex combination of thoughts, yet they can interact in seconds so you know what to do. This is what your gray matter—your cerebral cortex—does for you.

A Well-Oiled Machine—The Cerebellum

The cerebellum is a small, rounded part of the brain found in the back underneath the bulk of the cerebrum. It is only about $\frac{1}{10}$ of the brain, but it is a very important part. Its job is to make all your movements smooth without your having to think about it. Like an engine with many moving parts, the cerebellum helps your body put together balance and movement so you can do things. Think of all the muscles, nerves, and senses you need just to walk up stairs. Now how about climbing on the monkey bars? If your cerebellum was injured in an accident, every step you took from then on would be jerky and difficult. Your cerebellum keeps you running like a well-oiled machine with many moving parts.

The Brain Stem

The brain stem's job is to quietly take care of important bodily functions that you don't think about like heart rate, breathing, and even coughing. These are sometimes called lower functions, because you don't think about them. They just keep plugging along without your conscious help. Just because they are "lower" functions, though, doesn't mean they're not important. If anything happened to your brain stem, all your bodily functions would stop, including your heart! Plus, all the messages to and from the brain and body pass through the brain stem as well. In this case, the stem is just as important as the main fruit on top—the brain.

Extra Protection

The brain and spinal cord are surrounded by a protective cushion of fluid in which they float (called *cerebrospinal fluid*), and a tough layer of tissue around that called the *meninges*. These protect the brain and spinal cord from being banged around when you run and jump. If your brain does get banged, it is called a *concussion*. This can make you feel dizzy and even pass out. A bad concussion can damage your brain.

The Message Highway—The Spinal Cord

The spinal cord runs from the brain down to just below the ribs inside the protective bony canal of the vertebral column. It is the pathway for all the messages to and from the brain. From what you have read so far about the nervous system, can you tell what the spinal cord is made up of? It is the very long and very, very

Strokes and the Brain

When a person has a stroke, it means that a blood clot in one of the arteries in his brain blocks blood from getting to some parts of the brain. If there is no blood flow, then there is no oxygen and that part of the brain can actually die. Since your brain controls everything that you do, this would leave some things out of order! If the stroke happened in the area of your brain that controls speech, you would lose the ability to speak.

Health Tip

HOW A SEATBELT CAN SAVE YOUR BRAIN

The leading cause of death in accidents is from injuries to the brain when the head gets banged. That is why it is so important to wear a seatbelt in the car. If your head hits the windshield, it's a really big bang to the brain.

thin axons of millions and millions of nerve cells bringing their messages to and from the brain and body.

If the spinal cord is injured or broken, none of those important messages can come through to or from the brain. Your body below a break in the spinal cord cannot send signals to the brain, so you can't feel anything from that part of the body anymore. Your body below the break in the cord also cannot receive signals from the brain, so you can't move that part of the body anymore. This is called *paralysis* and can be permanent.

Emergency Reflexes

Sometimes a stimulus that needs a quick response—like accidentally grabbing a hot pan with your fingers—doesn't travel to the brain but instead just arcs around through the spinal cord to give a quicker response. This is called a *spinal reflex*. Pulling your hand away from a hot pan is a reflex and protects you from a burn without your brain even having to tell you what to do!

The Ins and Outs of the Peripheral Nervous System

The peripheral nervous system links the rest of your body to the spinal cord and brain. It does this coming and going. The information coming in is called the *sensory input*. The nerves bring the sensory input in to the spinal cord and brain (the central nervous system). When you wake up in the morning and see the light coming into your bedroom, that information is coming in through nerves to your brain. It is the same with the smell of bacon and the sound of your mother's call—smell and sound are picked up by nerves and brought to your brain, which makes sense of them for you.

The peripheral nervous system brings in messages from all over your body—from your skin, muscles, joints, and even your internal organs. If you eat too much food, you know it because you feel full. How do you know? The peripheral nerves are giving that message to your brain and your brain says—no more pie!

Carrying Out Your Brain's Orders

The second job of the peripheral nervous system is to carry signals going out—the motor output. If the brain wants to tell the muscles to get moving, it sends the signal out through the peripheral nerves to those muscles and off you go! Have you ever had to run for the school bus? It is the nerves in your peripheral nervous system that get the alarm from your brain and get your legs pumping.

Health Tip
UNHURRIED HEALING

If you cut a peripheral nerve in your arm or leg in an accident, you may get some paralysis from that spot to the end of your fingers or toes until the nerve grows back. Nerves grow very, very slowly though, so it may take a while. Scientists estimate that it can take as long as a month for every inch below the injury that the nerve axons have to grow back before you are all better. So be careful out there!

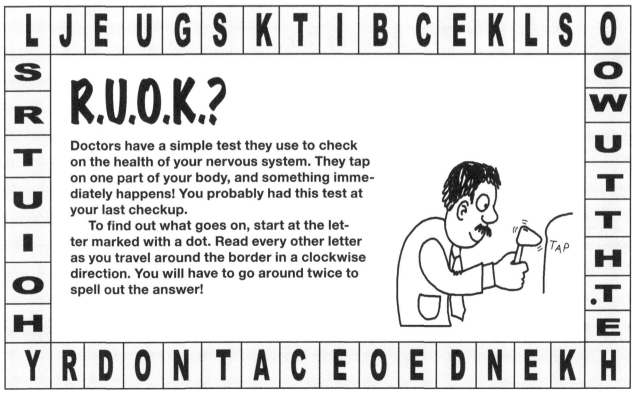

R.U.O.K.?

Doctors have a simple test they use to check on the health of your nervous system. They tap on one part of your body, and something immediately happens! You probably had this test at your last checkup.

To find out what goes on, start at the letter marked with a dot. Read every other letter as you travel around the border in a clockwise direction. You will have to go around twice to spell out the answer!

TAP

L J E U G S K T I B C E K L S O

S R T U I O H

O W U T T H T E

Y R D O N T A C E O E D N E K H

Fight or Flight

You don't control all of the motor output of your peripheral nervous system. Like your muscles, there are some you can control—the voluntary nervous system—and some you can't—the involuntary nervous system. Stop and scratch your nose. You just controlled both voluntary muscles and voluntary nervous system motor signals.

Have you ever had a friend grab you from behind or seen an angry dog rush up to the fence to bark at you? Your heart races and you gasp and jump. Sometimes you throw your arms up to protect yourself or even just turn and run. This is your involuntary nervous system at work. It controls all your everyday actions like heartbeat and digestion, but it also can give you a jolt of energy in an emergency. This is called the fight or flight reaction and it can save your life.

Some Nerve!

The thickest and largest nerve in the body is the sciatic nerve. It comes from the sacral nerves in the pelvis and runs down the back of your legs where it splits into two smaller nerves. The sciatic nerve gets messages from and reacts to things happening in your legs and feet.

It Takes Nerve

Peripheral nerves are broken down into different groups by where they are found:

- The peripheral nerves that come off your brain are called the **cranial nerves**. They get messages from and react to smells, eyesight, the mouth and face, hearing, the tongue and speech, and even some areas in the neck and abdomen.
- The peripheral nerves that come off the spinal cord in the neck are called the **cervical nerves**. They get messages from and react to things happening in the neck, arms, hands, shoulders, and diaphragm.
- The peripheral nerves that come off the spinal cord in the thorax are called **thoracic nerves**. They get messages from and react to things happening in the arms, hands, ribcage, chest, and upper back.

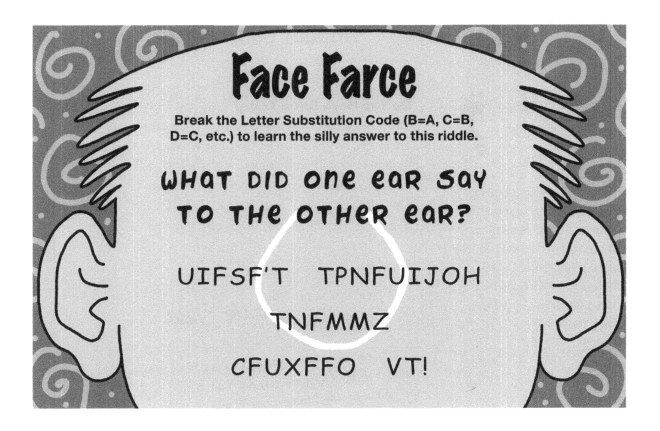

Face Farce

Break the Letter Substitution Code (B=A, C=B, D=C, etc.) to learn the silly answer to this riddle.

WHAT DID ONE EAR SAY TO THE OTHER EAR?

UIFSF'T   TPNFUIJOH

TNFMMZ

CFUXFFO   VT!

◆ The peripheral nerves that come off the spinal cord in the pelvis are called **lumbar nerves** and **sacral nerves**. They get messages from and react to things happening in the hips, buttocks, legs, and feet.

The Special Senses

The sensors you have to feel cold, heat, pain, and pressure are very important for your survival, but they are not your special senses. The special senses are sight, smell, taste, and hearing. Without them your life would be a lot duller. Each special sense is linked to peripheral nerves that lead right to the brain. These are also called cranial nerves. Their connection right to the brain leads to a very fast reaction time. This is a good thing, because these senses help protect you from dangers in the world.

FUN FACTS

Taste Bud Central

You might think that your tongue is one big taste center, but the truth is you have about 10,000 taste buds crammed onto your tongue to do all that tasting. And because eating is rough work, each taste bud only survives for about 7–10 days before being replaced.

Do You Have Good Taste?

The taste buds are the sensory receptors for taste. They are mostly found on the tongue. They are what give your tongue that rough feel. Each taste bud has tiny hairs that pick up signals from the foods you eat. When food mixes with saliva on your tongue, it bathes the taste buds, and the receptor hairs pick up the taste signal and send it on to your brain to enjoy.

Taste Test

It might be fun to test where your taste buds for different tastes are located on your tongue. You will need something sweet, salty, bitter, and sour. Try a tablespoon of sugar stirred into a cup of warm water, a tablespoon of salt stirred into a cup of warm water, ⅓ of a cup of vinegar, and a small amount of lemon squeezed into a cup. You will need an eyedropper or straw to get the flavors to the right areas of the tongue. Work with a partner and write down on a sheet of paper where you each tasted each of the flavors.

1. Use the eyedropper to place a drop of each flavor on the different areas of the tongue. If you cannot get an eyedropper, you can pull a few drops up with the straw by submerging it in the fluid and using your finger over the other end to keep some fluid in the straw, and then carefully drop a few drops on the tongue.
2. Repeat this on the 4 taste areas of the tongue.
3. Record which foods you could taste where on your tongue. Did your tongue have different areas from your partner?

There are 4 main tastes that your taste receptors pick up—sweet, sour, salty, and bitter. The taste buds that pick up these different tastes are found on different areas of the tongue. The tip of your tongue tastes mostly sweet and salty foods. The sides of your tongue pick up sour tastes and the back of your tongue picks up bitter tastes.

Good Smells and Bad Smells

Your sense of smell comes from a patch of receptors on the roof of the inside of your nose or nasal cavity. When you sniff a food, you bring its odor into the nasal cavity to bathe your smell receptors. Though taste and smell have separate sensors, taste depends a lot on your sense of smell. About 80 percent of what you taste comes from your smell sensors. For fine tastes, like the difference between a store-bought cupcake and a freshly baked, homemade chocolate cake, it helps to have a sense of smell.

Tasting with Your Nose

You and a friend can test how much of your taste comes from your nose. You will need an apple, pear, potato, knife, plate, and paper and pencil for writing down your results. You can ask a grownup to help you do the cutting-up part.

1. Cut up the apple, pear, and potato into small pieces.
2. Take turns blindfolding one of you to be the taster. The other will be the tester. The taster should then pinch his nose closed with one hand. He should make sure that he cannot see through his blindfold or breathe through his nose.
3. Then the tester should place a small slice of either pear, apple, or potato into the taster's mouth. The taster should guess which it is—pear, apple, or potato.
4. Try it several times, and each time the tester should write down the results.
5. Now try it again without holding your nose.
6. Compare how many times the taster got it right using help from his sense of smell. Do you see a pattern?

Seeing Is Believing

It's hard to imagine what life would be like without your ability to simply see the world around you, but your ability to see things is a lot more complex than you might think. On a sunny day when you look at a dog playing with a ball, do you know how you see it? Light reflects off the dog and enters your eye. It passes

FUN FACTS

Color-Blind?

Color blindness is when you are missing the cones for either red or green and see both as the same color. Many color-blind people don't even know they are color-blind until they are tested. It is much more common in boys than in girls.

TRY THIS

Can You See in the Dark?

Test your rods and cones. You will need to do this in a room that can be made very dark. Wait for your vision to adjust to the dark and look around. You will see things in the room, though they will not be very clear. You may know what color they are from memory, but can you actually see the colors in the dark? Try it out on a friend who doesn't know the room. Can they tell you the colors of things?

through your eye structures, which include your cornea, lens, the protective fluid inside your eyeball, and into your retina. The retina is made up of several layers of cells including the receptors for light—the photoreceptors. The photoreceptors come in two forms—rods and cones.

Rods and Cones

The rods in your eyes see things in dim light. They also see the things you glimpse on the very edge of your vision (your peripheral vision). Rods see things in black and white and not very sharply, but they are much more sensitive than cones are to light. That's why at night when your eyes adjust to the dark, you can make out the furniture enough not to run into it, but you can't tell what color it is or clearly see it.

Cones, on the other hand, see things in bright light. They see all the colors sharply. They don't, however, see anything in dim light. The rods and cones will send what they see—the visual stimulus—on to the brain. Your brain will then make sense of it so you can understand what you are seeing.

Do You Hear What I Hear?

The ears are not just for hearing. They also help you with balance and sensing the tilt of your head, but for now let's focus on hearing. The ears are designed inside and out for hearing. They have 3 parts—the outer, middle, and inner ear. The large outer ear (called the auricle) is what you see and helps direct sound waves into the ear canal. The ear canal ends at the eardrum, which vibrates when sound enters the ear.

The middle ear is a small space with the 3 smallest bones of the body. They are the *malleus* (called the hammer), the *incus* (called the anvil) and the *stapes* (called the stirrup). They receive and pass on the sound vibrations to the inner ear.

Parts of the Ear

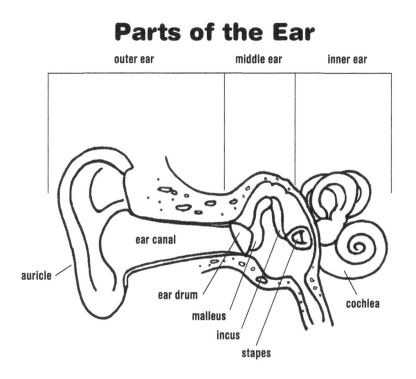

outer ear   middle ear   inner ear

auricle

ear canal

ear drum

malleus

incus

stapes

cochlea

Health Tip

DON'T BEAT THIS DRUM

To protect your hearing you should never put anything into your ear. Even a cotton swab meant for cleaning earwax should not be put inside your ear canal because it can puncture your eardrum. You also can destroy hearing receptors by listening to really loud music for a long time. Over time it can make you deaf. So turn down the music a bit and make everyone happier!

The inner ear is where the *cochlea*, a spiral-shaped chamber, houses the sound receptors. The sound receptors pass the sound on to the brain as an electrical signal and the brain tells you what you are hearing. This may sound like a long process, but it happens in less than a second!

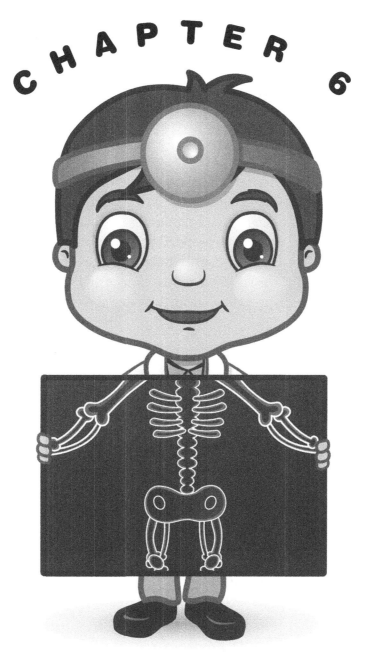

CHAPTER 6

KEEPING THE BALANCE—
THE ENDOCRINE SYSTEM

What Is a Hormone?

Like the nervous system, the endocrine system helps the body run smoothly. As a matter of fact, the nervous system and endocrine system work together to keep the body in balance. Instead of using electric signals like the nervous system, though, the endocrine system uses chemical substances to get the body to respond. Secreted by glands into the bloodstream, these chemical substances are called *hormones*. Hormones affect cells far away from where they are made and take longer to affect the body than a nerve impulse, but the reaction can last much longer, too.

What's a Gland?

Endocrine organs are glands. Compared to other organs in the body, endocrine glands can be tiny, sometimes no more than a few cells.

Some endocrine organs just do endocrine jobs, like the pituitary, thyroid, and adrenal glands. Other organs can be mixed, with some endocrine cells doing endocrine jobs and other cells doing other jobs of that organ system. These organs include the pancreas, intestines, ovaries, and testes.

Endocrine glands are found scattered all over the body and are very different from each other. They even have different jobs from each other. When a hormone reaches its target organ, it decides how the organ will act. It makes its target organ speed up or slow down, do more or do less.

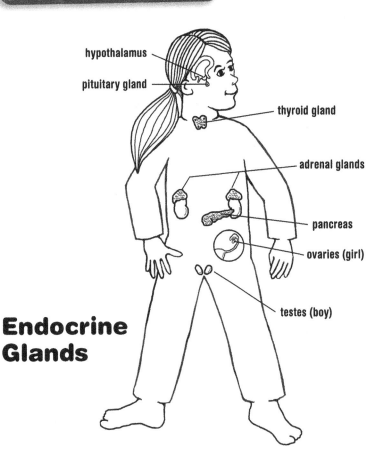

hypothalamus
pituitary gland
thyroid gland
adrenal glands
pancreas
ovaries (girl)
testes (boy)

Endocrine Glands

Hitting the Target

Endocrine glands release their hormones into the blood, but these hormones are very specific about which organs they affect. The target organs have receptors just for that hormone, so they are a perfect fit, like a lock and key. For example, if you are on a long hike and don't have enough water with you, your endocrine system is doing something about it. First, your brain senses that you are low on water. It tells your pituitary gland to secrete a hormone (called ADH) that tells your kidneys to keep as much water as possible. The kidneys will react by saving more water. If you still don't have enough water, your brain tells you to drink water. You get thirsty! The other effect you will notice is that you will not urinate as much as usual. This is because your endocrine system is making your body reuse the water it has, instead of telling you to get rid of it. Once you drink enough water, your brain tells your pituitary to stop making ADH and you are no longer thirsty. It is all done automatically by the body without you thinking about it—other than bringing water with you.

WORDS TO KNOW

endocrine

Endocrine glands secrete hormones directly into the blood. They are compared to exocrine glands, like sweat glands, that secrete through ducts out onto the skin.

The Master Glands

In a bony seat of your skull, in between the 2 hemispheres of your cerebrum, sits a tiny gland the size of a pea. This is the pituitary gland. For such a small organ, it is very powerful. It has sometimes been called the *master gland* because most of its hormones control other glands. But scientists now know that an area of the brain (called the *hypothalamus*) really controls the pituitary gland. This is how the brain controls your hormones. Still, the pituitary gland sends out at least 8 hormones that control other organs and glands throughout the body, so it is a very important endocrine gland.

Perfect Fit

Hormones are powerful chemical messengers that travel through the bloodstream. How do the hormone messages make something happen in just one body system if they are traveling all over the body? Each hormone fits its target like a key fits into a lock. The hormone will only affect the cells that they can chemically connect with! See if you can match each of these circling hormones with the proper target.

The Energy Gland—The Thyroid

The thyroid gland is a butterfly-shaped gland that sits in the front of your neck. It is the largest endocrine gland in the body and makes 3 hormones with very important jobs affecting your metabolism. One thyroid hormone (called thyroid hormone or TH) affects every cell in your body, telling them how fast to run things. If the thyroid sends out too much or too little TH it can have a big effect. Too much of this hormone causes the body to run too fast and hot. It makes you sleepless and anxious, with a pounding heart. Too little of this hormone causes the body to be cold, sluggish, and depressed. Just the right amount of hormones makes you healthy and keeps your body running smoothly. If you don't have enough of this hormone, doctors can give you a pill with TH that makes your thyroid hormone level normal.

WORDS TO KNOW

metabolism

All the chemical processes that happen inside your body to keep you alive are considered part of your metabolism.

The Pancreas and Sugar

The pancreas is actually 2 glands in 1. It contains some endocrine cells and some cells that just help with the digestion of food. The endocrine cells make *insulin*, a hormone that is important because it affects how much sugar, or *glucose*, is in the blood. That may not seem like a big deal, but without insulin, a person will die.

Here is why. After you eat, the food is broken down into its simplest form and taken into the blood, which delivers it to all your tissues to fuel everything you do. It is insulin's job to pull the blood sugar out of the blood and into your cells, where it is used to make energy. If the endocrine cells of the pancreas don't make and secrete insulin, the sugar stays in the blood and doesn't feed your hungry tissues. Instead, the sugar (glucose) is lost in the urine. The body thinks it's starving even though you are eating. To feed itself, the body will start to break down other tissues. Since the sugar does not go into the cells, it pours into the urine, a condition called *diabetes mellitus* (Type 1 diabetes), which means "sweet urine." The only treatment known for severe diabetes mellitus is regular shots of insulin.

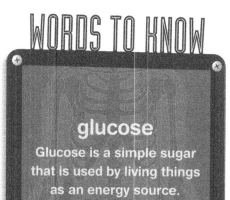

WORDS TO KNOW

glucose

Glucose is a simple sugar that is used by living things as an energy source.

People can develop diabetes if they are very overweight, or obese, especially if they become obese as children. In this situation, the pancreas makes insulin, but the cells of the body stop reacting to it. Since the sugars cannot get into the cells, it causes diabetes, though this type is called Type 2. Since obesity seems to trigger Type 2 diabetes in people, it is a good idea to keep your weight down, get exercise, and eat healthy foods. Diabetes is no fun.

FUN FACTS

Sweating Salt

Have you ever noticed that when you sweat it tastes salty, like the ocean? About 99 percent of your sweat is water pulled from your blood to help cool you off, but 1 percent is made up of your body's salts like sodium and other ions. So it tastes salty!

Other Glands and Their Jobs

There are many other important glands in the body. All of them work to make things run smoothly. Another important endocrine gland is the adrenal gland. There are actually 2 adrenal glands. Each one sits on top of one of your kidneys, like a cap. They make more than 20 hormones. Their jobs are to keep your heart rate, blood pressure, and energy levels normal. They also balance the amount of water, sodium, potassium, and other ions that are in your body. These ions are important for different jobs throughout your body, like muscle contractions and nerve impulses. If the ion levels in your blood get too low, your adrenal gland will release a hormone that tells your kidney to keep more sodium. Once you have enough sodium, you will stop releasing the hormone. Again, it's all automatic! Without hormones from your adrenal gland, your body would not function.

Girls and Boys Growing Up

The reproductive organs also contain endocrine glands that control how we grow up and mature into adults. In girls, the endocrine glands for reproduction are the *ovaries*. In boys, the endocrine glands for reproduction are the *testes*. These endocrine glands are with you since birth, but they are not really doing much all throughout your childhood. They begin to become active when you are between 10 and 15 years old. This is called *puberty* and is marked by changes in your body toward adulthood. This is all controlled by your brain, which tells the pituitary gland to make the hormones that act on your ovaries or testes. You will learn more about them in Chapter 10.

Crossed Messages

There are over 50 different hormones swirling through your body and carrying messages that help control many, many important body functions! See if you can fit all the functions listed here into their proper places in the criss-cross grid.

BLOOD
BODY
CALCIUM
DIGESTION
ENERGY
GROWTH
HEART
IMMUNE
INSULIN
MOOD
REPRODUCTION
SALT
SLEEP

cycles

R

temperature   Y

rate   T   O

O   U

pressure   system   levels

I   levels

They're everywhere!

How Hormone Levels Are Controlled in the Body

Too much or too little of any hormone can have a bad effect on the body. Like the story of the 3 bears, the body needs an amount of hormones that is just right. So when the body has had enough of a hormone, it has a system for stopping the glands from sending out any more. It is called the *negative feedback system.*

The negative feedback system is simple. Hormones are released from a gland when it senses that the body needs them. This is usually triggered by a stimulus like not having enough water or having too much salt. Also, the pancreas releases insulin after you eat because it senses a lot of sugar entering the blood as you're digesting the food in your intestine. Then the insulin begins to help the sugar in your blood go into your cells to fuel your tissues. Soon, the sugar levels in your blood go down again. The levels get so low that the pancreas stops getting its blood sugar stimulus. This stops it from releasing any more insulin. This feedback told the cells of your pancreas that there was no more blood sugar to deal with. So it stopped shipping out insulin. The negative feedback system really works!

When Good Glands Go Bad—Gland Problems

Because hormones have such important jobs, when a gland isn't working right it can cause a lot of problems for the body. As you read previously, weight issues can interfere with insulin production, causing diabetes, but there are other gland problems that can occur as well.

A problem with the release of growth hormone (GH) from the pituitary gland can also have an effect on a person. If not enough

Record Holder
The shortest woman on earth was from the Netherlands and reached only 2 feet tall. She only lived to be 19 years old.

Big Foot
The biggest feet on earth belong to a giant American who wears a size 29½ shoe. He is 7 feet and 6 inches tall. He is not the tallest man on earth, though. That record belongs to a man who grew to 8 feet and 11 inches tall!

growth hormone is released in a growing child, she can develop dwarfism and never grow above 4 feet tall.

If too much growth hormone is released in a growing child, she can develop gigantism. Giants are abnormally tall. They have normal body proportions but look really big, sometimes growing more than 8 feet tall!

Scientists have developed many synthetic hormones in the laboratory to treat people with glands that are not working. This has made life easier for those with malfunctioning endocrine glands.

Adding Iodine

To work properly, the thyroid gland needs the element iodine. Without it, the gland can get out of whack and swell into a huge lump called a "goiter." In 1924, a group of food producers started adding iodine to their product to prevent goiters and help the public stay healthy. You can still find iodine in this product today! Connect the dots on the carton to find the name of this familiar food.

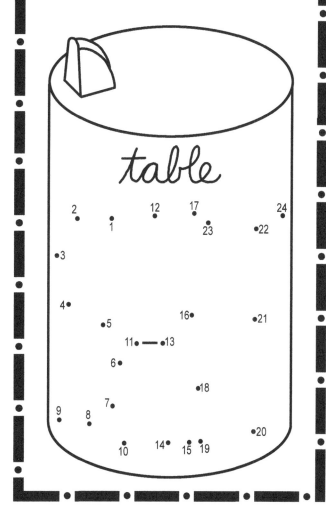

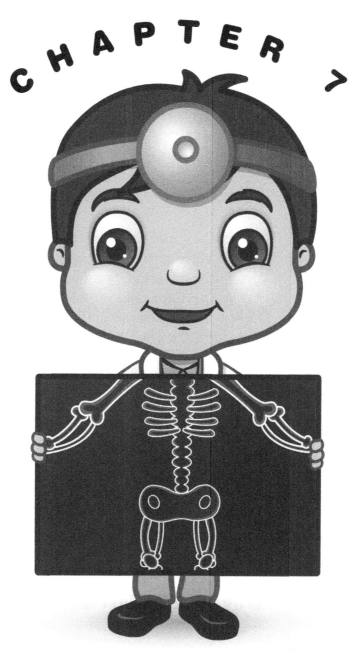

CHAPTER 7

LET'S CIRCULATE—
THE CIRCULATORY SYSTEM

What Is Blood?

Blood may seem like just a solid red liquid, but it's really made up of many different kinds of cells floating in a fluid called *plasma*. Blood is also a tissue because like other tissues, it is made up of different kinds of cells with a similar function—but it is the only liquid tissue.

Blood is considered connective tissue, except that it has no fibers in it like other connective tissues. Only when blood begins to clot do fibrin strands begin to show up in it. Blood has 3 kinds of cells—red blood cells, white blood cells, and platelets. There are way more red blood cells than any other kind of blood cells. There are 800 red blood cells for every 1 white blood cell found in your blood. The liquid plasma of your blood is clear and makes up more than half of all your blood.

Looking at Your Blood

Sometimes a doctor will take a blood sample and spin it in a machine so that the denser parts go to the bottom. The doctor does this to separate out the blood cells. The densest cells are the red blood cells. They pile up at the bottom of the test tube. Then there is a small white layer of the white blood cells and tiny platelets. Then all the plasma sits on top.

Why Do You Have Blood?

Most importantly, blood is a built-in delivery system, bringing things to all your tissues from your nose to your toes. Here are some of the important things your blood does:

- It delivers oxygen to your tissues and gets rid of carbon dioxide.
- It delivers nutrients and gets rid of waste.
- It delivers hormones from their glands to their target organs.

FUN FACTS

Weighing In on Blood
Blood makes up about 8 percent of your body weight. So if you weigh 100 pounds, you have 8 pounds of blood. A 200-pound man has as much as 16 pounds of blood.

◆ It keeps your body temperature uniform by picking up heat from warm muscles and spreading it out evenly throughout the body.

◆ It helps defend the body from illnesses by delivering white blood cells to the site of an injury or infection so they can fix things.

◆ It seals itself off when you bleed after an injury by clotting.

Blood is an amazing tissue!

Blood Cells at Work

The blood's cells each have their own important job to do. Red blood cells pick up oxygen in the lungs and bring it all around the body. All your body's cells need a constant supply of oxygen to survive, so this is a very important job. The red blood cells also pick up the waste, like carbon dioxide, from the cells and bring it back to the lungs so you can exhale it out of your body.

Health Tip
WHERE'S THE BEEF?

Sometimes people get a condition where their body does not have enough red blood cells. This is called *anemia*. Because they lack enough red blood cells to deliver oxygen, they feel tired and have low energy. Anemia can happen for many reasons, but sometimes it is from a poor diet with not enough iron. Iron comes in foods like red meat and dark green leafy vegetables. Girls often have fewer red blood cells than boys, so they should especially make sure they eat right!

Heart and Lungs

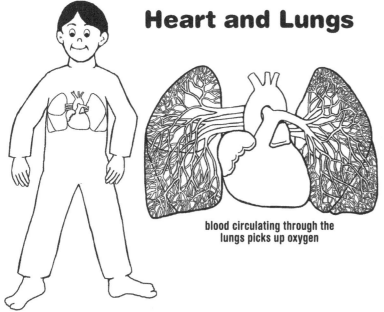

blood circulating through the
lungs picks up oxygen

If your cells need more oxygen than they are getting, even with your heart pumping fast, your body will make more red blood cells to help out. This happens in athletes who are working out a lot, or someone visiting high altitudes (where oxygen is thinner), or someone who loses blood in an accident. But even in normal people, the body makes about 2 million red blood cells every second!

Your Very Own Superheroes

You have many fewer white blood cells than red blood cells. White blood cells only make up about 1 percent of your blood, but they are powerful! They fight off the diseases that attack your body like little superheroes. They can kill viruses, bacteria, cancer, and parasites. Like superheroes, they have special powers. White blood cells can actually leave the blood and go into your tissues. Once there, they can help fix injured and infected tissues.

If you have ever had an infected cut that got red and swollen with pus, your white blood cells came to the rescue to cushion and treat the injured area. You should know that for every cold virus or other infection you have ever gotten, your white blood cells have fought off many, many more that you never even knew about.

Your Body's Bandage Bits

The other cells in your blood are *platelets* and are not really true cells at all, but bits of bigger cells. Platelets are very important because they help with blood clotting, which stops the bleeding after you are injured. If your blood didn't clot properly, like in a person with hemophilia, every small cut could be a life-threatening injury. Platelets are always in the blood in case you get a cut. They are attracted to a wound and will stick like glue to the spot, forming a protective clot until the tissue heals. Every time you get a cut and a scab, you can see your platelets at work.

WORDS TO KNOW

pus

Pus is a whitish fluid that surrounds an infected injury. It is full of white blood cells that gave their lives to fight your infection.

What's Your Type?

If you looked at red blood cells under a powerful microscope, you would see protein molecules on the surface. Doctors use these proteins to separate blood into four groups: A, B, AB, and O. If you ever need to get extra blood because of surgery or an injury, your doctor will make sure you get the type that matches the blood already in your body!

   Use the clues and grid to figure out what blood type each of the four children have. Hint: Each blood type is only used one time.

Barb's blood type is not two letters.

Sam's blood type does not have a B in it.

Lily's blood type is a single letter, but not O.

Sam's blood type is not O.

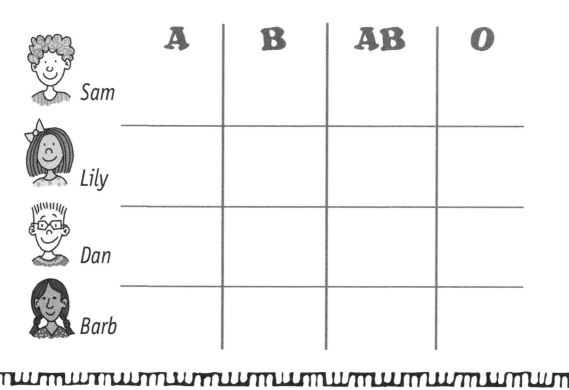

	A	B	AB	O
Sam				
Lily				
Dan				
Barb				

WORDS TO KNOW

hemophilia

Hemophilia is a genetic disease where the blood cannot clot because 1 of the clotting factors is missing. This is a very serious illness. Until recently, when scientists were able to make clotting factors in the laboratory, most people with hemophilia did not live a very long life.

Giving Blood

Hospitals need extra blood for patients all the time. They need it for people who have been in accidents and lose a lot of blood. They need it for people having surgery who may need extra blood. In general, any person may need to get blood at some time in his or her life. Hospitals and blood banks can store blood for several weeks. So it's always a good idea to donate some of your blood when you are old enough to spare some. You never know when you might need some extra blood yourself!

You Gotta Have Heart

Though you can't live without it, the heart is really just a pump that keeps your blood going around and around your body, through tubes called *arteries*, delivering oxygen and food to all your tissues. For such an important organ, your heart is small—it weighs less than a pound and is no bigger than a fist. It is made

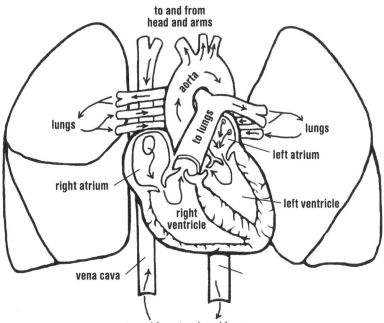

of mostly muscle, which makes it well suited for its job. It must squeeze down hard—or contract—to give the blood a mighty push, sending it through to its next destination.

The heart is covered by many protective layers. First, it is inside a double-layered sac made of tough fibers. This sac also helps anchor the heart in place while it's pumping. To its right and left, the heart is protected and enclosed by the lungs. In back lies the bony vertebral column. In front lies the sternum. The heart sits on top of the diaphragm, the big sheet of muscle that rises and falls when you breathe. That's a lot of protection for one of our most important organs.

Your Beating Heart

The heart has 4 rooms, called chambers. The 2 smaller chambers on top are the *atria*. The 2 larger chambers on bottom are the *ventricles*. There is a front door and back door in each chamber. The doors, called heart valves, help move the blood through the heart and lungs. The front door snaps shut after enough blood flows into the chamber. Then the chamber builds pressure. Then the back door pops open and the chamber pumps its blood out in a surge on to its next stop. Every time the doors (heart valves) snap shut, you hear it as a heartbeat. The familiar lub-dub heart sounds are the heart valves snapping shut behind moving blood.

Except for your heartbeat, blood flows silently though all the chambers of your heart. Sometimes, though, one of your heart's valves may not close all the way and blood will swish back through it. Or a valve won't open all the way so the blood spurts through it, like when you put your thumb over the end of a flowing hose. These changes in blood flow cause unusual sounds that are called heart murmurs. A doctor can hear a heart murmur in a regular checkup. In most cases, a murmur will not hurt you, but every once in a while a heart murmur will be serious enough to need surgery. It's always a good idea to get regular checkups throughout your life, just in case.

A Whale of a Heart
Animals have hearts that suit their size. A whale's heart needs to be big enough to pump blood to all its tissues. For an animal the size of a school bus, that would have to be a pretty big heart. As a matter of fact, the blue whale's heart is as big as a Volkswagen Beetle!

Listening to Your Heart
You can easily hear someone's heartbeat without any of the tools your doctor has. Have your dad lie on the couch. Turn off the TV or other sounds in the room. Lay your ear on the middle of his chest, over his bony sternum. Block any other sounds from entering your other ear by covering it with your hand. Can you hear the lub-dub sounds? Those are your dad's heart valves working!

WORDS TO KNOW

oxygenate

To oxygenate something is simply to supply it with oxygen. When the blood is oxygenated in the lungs, it means that the blood picks up the oxygen you inhale, which is then delivered to the body.

The Right and Left Heart

The blood's pathway through the heart is really 2 pathways. That is because by the time the blood reaches the heart, it has had most of its oxygen taken out by the tissues and it is now loaded with carbon dioxide waste. So first the blood must be pumped through the lungs, drop off its carbon dioxide load, and pick up some new oxygen. That is done by the right side of the heart. When the blood returns from the lungs, it goes through the left side of the heart and then back out to the body to deliver its fresh load of oxygen. This may sound like a long process, but it happens literally in a heartbeat.

High Tide

When you listen to a seashell, you hear the sound of the ocean, right? Since the ocean isn't actually inside the shell, what are you really hearing? Start at the outermost letter on the shell. Read every other letter as you spiral into the middle. Then turn around and continue reading every other letter on the way out. They will spell the answer!

What are you really hearing when you listen to a seashell?

The Path Through the Heart

This is how the blood travels through the heart:

1. First, the blood comes into the right atrium of the heart from the body.
2. Next, it passes through a valve into the right ventricle.
3. Then it is pumped through a valve to the lungs where it picks up oxygen. This is called being oxygenated.
4. Next, it flows back through a valve into the left atrium.
5. Then it passes through a valve into the left ventricle.
6. The left ventricle is the most muscular chamber because it must squeeze down with a mighty contraction to thrust the blood on its way throughout the body.
7. Off it goes!

The Blood Vessels

The blood vessels in your body bring the blood to and from your heart in one long, continuous circle. They may look a bit like the plumbing system in your house because they are tubes that start big at the heart and grow smaller and smaller as they reach their destination in the tissues. However, there are a few big differences:

- The circulatory system is a closed system, beginning and ending at the heart and just circling around and around and around.
- Blood vessels can expand and narrow when the body needs more or less blood flow.
- Blood vessels repair themselves when damaged! Every single bleeding cut you ever got was the result of a torn blood vessel. Luckily, they do heal over time and go back to work.
- Your body can grow extra blood vessels when an area needs more blood flow.

Health Tip

HOW TO AVOID A HEART ATTACK

Some 250,000 Americans die from a heart attack every year. There are many things you can do as you grow up to keep your heart healthy:

* Get regular exercise. Your heart is a muscle and needs to be kept in shape.
* Keep your weight down. The heavier you are, the harder your heart needs to work.
* Eat good food. A healthy, low-fat diet will not only help you keep your weight down but will keep your heart and blood vessels healthy.
* Don't smoke. Cigarette smoking weakens the heart and blood vessels and contributes to heart attacks.
* When you grow up, don't drink a lot of alcohol. Like cigarettes, too much alcohol raises the chances of a heart attack.
* Try to relax. Stress is not good for your body in general. In between working, make time for your body and mind to relax.
* If your grandparents or parents have had heart attacks, get regular check-ups when you grow up so you and your doctor know your heart is still healthy.

Arteries from Your "Heart-eries"

There are 3 main kinds of blood vessels: arteries, veins, and capillaries. The arteries carry blood away from the heart. Usually that means the blood in the arteries is full of oxygen, and in most cases this is true. The 1 exception is the blood leaving the heart to go to the lungs to get oxygenated.

The biggest artery in the body is the *aorta*. It leaves the left ventricle of the heart and arches up toward the brain, then down through the chest and abdomen, giving off smaller branches along the way to all your internal organs like your stomach, kidneys, liver, muscles, and intestines. The aorta is so big that it actually needs blood vessels of its own to feed it.

Arteries are made up of layers, including a layer of muscle. The muscle layer allows the artery to squeeze down tight to slow blood flow and raise your blood pressure if the body asks for it. It can also expand the artery if you need more blood flow to some part of your body. An example of this is when you are exercising and your body increases blood flow to your muscles. After a big meal your body will increase blood flow to your intestines.

The Arteries

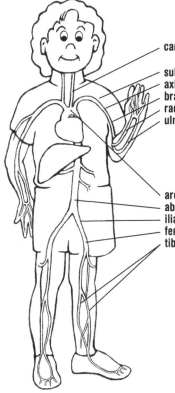

carotid artery (to head)

subclavian artery (in shoulder) becomes
axillary (in armpit) which becomes
brachial artery (in upper arm) then splits into
radial artery (to outside of arm) and
ulnar artery (to inside of arm)

arch of the aorta becomes
abdominal aorta (to organs) then splits to
iliac arteries (to pelvic region) and become
femoral artery (to legs) then splits into
tibial arteries (to legs and feet)

The Tiny Capillaries

The blood from your heart travels along smaller and smaller arteries to reach every inch of your body. Finally it will enter your tiny capillaries. The capillaries are the smallest blood vessels in your body and can be as thin as 1 cell thick. That is because this is where the blood vessel drops off its oxygen and food load and picks up the carbon dioxide waste. Oxygen, carbon dioxide, and nutrients can pass right through the thin-walled capillaries. Most tissues in your body are rich with capillaries feeding them.

There and Back Again—The Vein Train

After the capillaries have traded their oxygen for carbon dioxide, it is time to go back to the heart. They will send their blood back through tiny veins that feed into larger and larger veins until they reach the biggest vein in the body—the *vena cava*. The vena cava empties its blood back into the atrium on the right side of the heart.

Blood Vessels–Free Zone

Only a few tissues in the body have few or no blood vessels at all. These include cartilage, tendons, and ligaments. This makes them heal more slowly if they are torn, because they will need to get their vital nutrients from nearby tissues that do have blood vessels of their own.

Leaky Valves

By the time blood reaches the veins, the pumping action of the heart has gotten pretty weak. In addition to that, the blood in veins has to climb against gravity to reach the heart. So the large veins have valves along the way back to the heart. This keeps the blood from falling back between blood-pumping heartbeats. Walking and moving your legs also squeezes your veins, helping to move the blood forward. Sometimes the valves get leaky as we age and the venous blood will flow back and pool down in the legs. This makes the leg veins bulge, their bluish blood showing through the skin. This is called varicose veins.

WORDS TO KNOW

nutrient
A nutrient is something that is used by the body to help with growth, ongoing needs, and repairs.

FUN FACTS

The Long Road
Altogether, the blood vessels travel more then 60,000 miles inside your body. That's a lot of plumbing!

The Heart Needs Oxygen, Too

Even the heart has tiny blood vessels to feed it oxygen. The heart's muscle needs a lot of oxygen because it works so hard and never stops. As we age, fat debris builds up in our heart arteries, and the openings for blood to pass through get smaller and smaller. If they are blocked, oxygen cannot get to the heart, and the heart literally suffocates and dies. The result is a heart attack and can be fatal!

Stop Bleeding! Why You Scab

So you've cut yourself and you're bleeding. Ouch! It hurts and there is blood leaking out. Don't panic. Your body is already working on repairing the damage. Wash the area with soap and water, pat it dry, and cover it snugly with a bandage. Over the next few days your body will be very busy working on that spot to fix it. This is what will happen:

1. The damaged blood vessels send out a signal that says, "We're hurt, send help!"
2. Blood cells (platelets), and blood proteins (fibrinogen), rush to the area. This trigger the platelets around the cut to thicken, and fibers suddenly appear in it. Your blood forms a clot that plugs up the hole in the blood vessels and clings to the edges of your cut skin.
3. The clot blocks any more blood from flowing out. Over the next couple of hours it will harden.
4. A scab has formed. It covers and protects the injured area while the body repairs it.
5. Any invading bacteria are destroyed.
6. Dead and injured cells are carried off by white blood cells.
7. The injured area becomes a little swollen, which cushions the injury and helps with the healing process.

WORDS TO KNOW

platelets

Platelets are small bits of cells found in the blood that help with clotting when you cut yourself.

fibrinogen

Fibrinogen is a substance in the blood that turns into stringy fibers when your blood clots and helps to form a scab.

8. The edges of the wound change and begin to bind together.

9. The cut blood vessels heal.

10. The scab falls off.

11. The skin heals, though with a bad cut it can sometimes leave a scar.

Your skin is healed! Be more careful.

Heart Troubles

Though the heart is a well-designed organ, made just right for what it does, sometimes things can go wrong and cause problems with your powerful pump. Before you are born, your blood does not have to circulate to your lungs, since you are inside your mother and are not breathing air yet. Because of this, before you are born, your blood goes right through your heart without ever going to your lungs at all. To make this easier, there is an opening between the 2 atria of your heart. So the blood goes right on through, without taking the detour through your right ventricle and your lungs. You can survive on this because you are getting oxygen from your mother through the umbilical cord.

After you are born and take your first breath, the doorway between the 2 atria grows and closes forever. That way the blood has to go into the lungs where it can pick up the oxygen you breathe. In some people, however, that doorway doesn't quite close. Some blood leaks through without going to the lungs and getting oxygen. This creates a murmur that your doctor can hear. It also means your heart is pumping out some blood that still carries the carbon dioxide waste you should be getting rid of in your lungs. It has no oxygen to feed your hungry tissues. Your body needs that oxygen to grow and exercise. A heart surgeon will have to go into the heart and fix it. He will close that little door and seal it for good. Then the body, with its healthy load of oxygen, can finally grow normally.

WORDS TO KNOW

clot

A clot is a thick mass of blood that has turned from a liquid into more of a soft solid, so it will not flow anymore.

Health Tip

FRENCH FRIES— A DEADLY WEAPON

Some foods are especially bad for the heart if you eat them regularly. Foods that are deep fat–fried, like French fries, can be artery clogging. Over a lifetime of eating these foods, the arteries can actually become blocked and the blood flow to the heart will stop. This is one factor that leads to heart attacks. Fatty foods can also add to obesity, which makes the heart have to work too hard. It is always better to eat fresh fruits and vegetables, grains, beans, and lean meats for a healthy heart.

CHAPTER 8

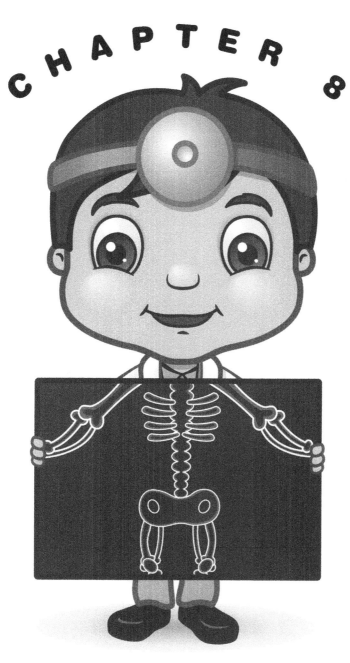

A BREATH OF FRESH AIR

WORDS TO KNOW

respiration

Respiration is the process of moving oxygen from the air you breathe into your body and carbon dioxide from your body into the air. This is done by breathing. Oxygen, which is needed to change the foods you eat into energy to run the body, is turned into carbon dioxide when you make energy. Using oxygen to make energy is also part of respiration.

WORDS TO KNOW

resonate

Your nose is like a resonating chamber, making your voice fuller and deeper. This means that it allows the sound of your voice to bounce around and vibrate to get bigger.

Why You Need Air

Your body is made up of trillions of cells. Each and every cell needs a never-ending supply of oxygen to run its daily job. Some cells, like those in your brain, cannot go for even a few minutes without oxygen or they will die. That is why you need oxygen every second. You can go without water for a few days and food for a couple of weeks, if you have to, but not oxygen. That you need now! In addition to needing oxygen, there is another important reason why you need to keep breathing. You have to get rid of carbon dioxide, a waste that will otherwise build up and poison your body. Respiration is very important.

Breaking Breathing Down

There are actually 4 parts to the process of respiration:

1. First, you bring the air in and out of your lungs. This is called *ventilation*.
2. Then, in your lungs you trade oxygen for carbon dioxide with your blood. This is called *external respiration*.
3. Next your blood brings the oxygen to all your cells. This is called *transport*.
4. Then the blood trades its load of oxygen for the cells' carbon dioxide waste. This is called *internal respiration*.

This process goes on all the time, over and over and over and over again, every minute, every hour, every day of your life.

The Breathing Pathway

To get the vital oxygen into all your cells, first you have to get it to your lungs. Every time you inhale, oxygen follows this pathway to get to your lungs.

1. First the oxygen passes into and through your nose.
2. Then it passes down the back of your throat. This area is called the *pharynx*.
3. Then it passes through the voice box, also called the *larynx*.
4. Then it passes through the windpipe, also called the *trachea*.
5. Then when the trachea splits into 2 tubes, called the *bronchi*, it goes through them into the lungs.
6. The oxygen follows the bronchi as they break down into smaller and smaller passageways in the lungs, eventually becoming the smallest airways—the *bronchioles*.
7. The bronchioles then get even smaller and end in tiny air sacs throughout the lungs called *alveoli*.
8. It is in the alveoli where the gas exchange happens—the oxygen passes into the blood and the carbon dioxide passes out of it.

So Nosey

Your nose is the only part of the respiratory system that you can see. It plays an important role. When you inhale air (which has oxygen in it), it is pulled into your nose from the outside world. It is usually cold, dry, and full of dust and germs. The inside of your nose warms the air and adds some moisture to it. The moist lining of your nose acts like a filter with tiny hairs that catch and trap dust and other particles that shouldn't go into your lungs. Though it isn't part of respiration, your nose also houses the smell receptors, so you can get an idea of where the oxygen you are breathing has been. The nose even plays a part in how your voice sounds. It acts as a sound chamber adding strength to your voice—this is called making your voice *resonate*.

TRY THIS

Disguising Your Voice

You can change the sound of your voice by squeezing down on your nose. This closes down the resonating chamber that makes your voice into the full, deep sound that it is. Try it. Pinch your nose with your fingers and say something. Sounds different, doesn't it? This shows you how much your nose does to make you sound the way you do.

Your Nose Is Running . . .

You breathe in the viruses and bacteria that are floating in the air all the time. Often they are trapped and destroyed, but sometimes they bother the lining of the nose so much that it begins to send out fluids called mucus. This is what makes your nose run. The mucus can run down your throat, too. It tickles your throat lining, making you cough. You have caught a cold. It's a good idea to blow your nose and get that mucus out and into the trash. It is also important to use a tissue when you sneeze or cough. Coughing and sneezing can push thousands of germs into the air. If other people breathe these germs in, they can get sick, too. Then wash your hands. The germs in your mucus can be passed on to other people from your hands. You don't want to get your friends or other people in your family sick!

Keeping Food Out of Your Airways

The air with its load of oxygen comes in your nose and mouth and flows down into your throat (pharynx), through your voice box (larynx), and into your windpipe (trachea). This is the same pathway that food takes when you eat, except that instead of going into your voice box, food is sent into another tube called the *esophagus* toward your stomach. Food is kept out of your voice box because when you swallow, a hard flap called the *epiglottis* flips down to cover the opening into your voice box, protecting it. You do not want anything other than oxygen to go into your lungs!

The Job of Coughing

Like the nose, the windpipe also has mucus to catch dust and particles. It also has tiny hairs that move in a wave to bring the mucus with the particles up away from the lungs. This is added protection to keep things out of the lungs. Smoking will ruin those hairs and make a lot more mucus, so the only way smokers can get rid of things caught in all the mucus of their windpipe is by coughing. This is called a "smoker's hack" and is a sign that

Health Tip

THOSE IMPORTANT NOSE HAIRS!

The tiny little hairs that line the inside of your nose trap dust and germs as they pass through. This protects your lungs from damage and your body from some of the germs that might make you sick. When people smoke cigarettes, the smoke over time will actually kill those important nose hairs. Once the hairs are gone, germs and dust can enter your lungs and your body. This is another great reason to never smoke cigarettes.

FUN FACTS

That Air Is Dry!

It is the job of your nose and nasal lining to add some moisture to the air you breathe. That's why if you breathe through your mouth for a while, your throat gets dry. That air needs some moisture added!

Coughing Speed

When you cough, the muscles in your windpipe contract so forcefully that the air shoots out of you at 60 miles per hour!

a smoker has done damage to his respiratory system. If he quits smoking, this protective system can recover over time.

It Pays to Be Sensitive

There is one last area that protects the lungs from things like specks of food and inhaled water that may get past the voice box and windpipe. Right where the trachea splits into the 2 bronchi, before they go into each lung, there is a sensitive area called the *carina*. The carina is the most sensitive spot of the entire respiratory system. If you inhale something that gets past all the other protective areas, when it hits the carina, it makes you cough violently. This is meant as a last resort to keep anything other than air out of your lungs.

Don't Get Choked Up

If you accidentally take a breath when you are swallowing, you may inhale a bit of food. This can happen if you are laughing or talking while eating. Food in your voice box will stimulate the cough reflex. This makes you cough sharply. It may be enough to throw out the bit of food. In the worst case, the food may lodge in your windpipe and block all air from getting through. This is choking —it is very serious and can kill a person.

A simple rescue someone can do on a choking person is to hug him or her sharply from behind to force the air out of the lungs in one pop. This often will shoot the stuck bit of food right out of the body. This is called the Heimlich maneuver and has saved many lives. Everyone should learn how to do the Heimlich maneuver just in case of emergency.

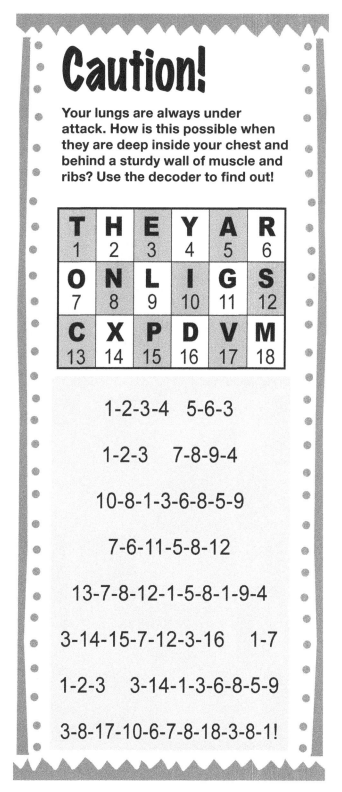

Caution!

Your lungs are always under attack. How is this possible when they are deep inside your chest and behind a sturdy wall of muscle and ribs? Use the decoder to find out!

T	H	E	Y	A	R
1	2	3	4	5	6
O	N	L	I	G	S
7	8	9	10	11	12
C	X	P	D	V	M
13	14	15	16	17	18

1-2-3-4 5-6-3

1-2-3 7-8-9-4

10-8-1-3-6-8-5-9

7-6-11-5-8-12

13-7-8-12-1-5-8-1-9-4

3-14-15-7-12-3-16 1-7

1-2-3 3-14-1-3-6-8-5-9

3-8-17-10-6-7-8-18-3-8-1!

The Bronchial Tree

When the windpipe (trachea) divides into the 2 bronchi, these are the first branches of the bronchial tree. The tubes of the bronchial tree stay open all the time because they contain a type of bone called cartilage. It is called the bronchial tree because its branching shape looks a bit like a tree, though it really would be an upside-down tree.

Like a tree, the bronchi divide again and again into smaller and smaller airways, the smallest being the bronchioles. Branching off the bronchioles are the tiny alveoli that cluster at the end of the airways like tiny bunches of grapes. Each bunch of grapes is called an *alveolar sac*. Each alveoli is a tiny chamber where oxygen is traded for carbon dioxide with the blood. Unlike the tubes of the bronchial tree, the alveoli have no cartilage and can stretch like a balloon when you breathe in.

That's a Lot of Grapes!
Scientists think that there are more than 400 million tiny grape-like alveoli in your lungs.

The Bronchial Tree

bronchiole

CO_2

red blood cells
inside a capillary

O_2

alveoli

How Oxygen Gets Into Your Blood

So far you have learned how your blood circulates around your body, dropping off oxygen and picking up carbon dioxide. Then it comes to the lungs and drops off its carbon dioxide and picks up oxygen, starting the cycle all over again. But how does it actually accomplish this amazing act?

By the time the blood vessels reach the alveoli in your lungs, they are tiny capillaries. The capillaries attach themselves right to the alveoli. They form a cobweb over them. The alveoli are balloon-shaped and have a lot of area for the capillaries to cover. The walls of both the alveoli and the capillaries are very, very thin—thinner than the paper on which these words are printed. Together they make up the respiratory membrane. On one side of the membrane is the oxygen and on the other side the blood is flowing by, full of carbon dioxide. Since there is more oxygen in the alveoli than in the blood, it moves across the thin respiratory membrane into the blood by a process called *diffusion*. Since there is more carbon dioxide in the blood than in the alveoli, it also moves by diffusion but in the opposite direction, across the membrane into the alveoli. This is how oxygen flows into the blood and the carbon dioxide flows into the alveoli. The gas exchange is done! Next, you exhale the carbon dioxide and inhale more oxygen. Your red blood cells take up the oxygen and off they go to deliver it throughout the body. This happens constantly, with every breath you take.

WORDS TO KNOW

diffusion

Diffusion is the spreading out of a gas until it is uniform everywhere. In other words, the oxygen flows from the blood into the alveoli because there is more oxygen in the blood than in the alveoli. Diffusion seeks to make the amount in both places equal, so it flows across the membrane.

WORDS TO KNOW

respiratory membrane

The respiratory membrane is the fused wall of the alveoli and the capillary lying next to it. It is across this membrane that oxygen is traded for carbon dioxide.

How Breathing Works

You breathe in and out—inhaling and exhaling—but it is not as simple as it sounds. There are many things that help you get the vital oxygen you need way down deep into your lungs.

Your lungs are actually attached to the inside of your ribcage. They are also attached on the bottom to your diaphragm, a strong, dome-shaped muscular sheet, on which they sit. Your lungs are

In and Out

Every day you do something important. And you don't do it just one time — you do it many, many times! What is it? To find the answer to this riddle, fill in the blanks with the numbers that answer each question. Add these numbers up and write the total in the empty box. Finally, break the Vowel Switch code to get the rest of the answer!

# of your organs that sense smell _____

# of ears on your body _____

# of digits on two hands and one foot _____

# of navels on your body _____

# of chambers in your heart _____

YEI BRUOTHU OBEIT

THEISOND TAMUS O DOY!

very elastic—like a balloon. You can picture your lungs like an empty balloon with only one opening at the top—the windpipe. When you take a breath, several things happen:

1. The diaphragm contracts, flattening out and pulling the lungs down. This happens when you are resting, without even thinking about it.
2. The muscles between your ribs can also contract, pulling your ribcage, and your lungs attached to them, outward. This happens when you are running or playing hard and your body needs more oxygen, or if you decide to take a deep breath.
3. Both these muscle contractions expand your lungs and make the space inside them bigger.
4. The bigger space inside your lungs causes a pressure change that draws the air into them to fill the space. This is how you inhale!

Waiting to Exhale

Your lungs are so elastic that after you inhale, your muscles relax and your ribcage sinks back down and your lungs automatically shrink back to their original size, pushing your breath out. Sometimes you need to force air out. This takes some muscles helping out. They force the ribcage down and the diaphragm up. This shrinks the lungs quickly and pushes the breath out with force. You do this when you whistle, sing, shout, or just blow out the birthday candles!

Make a Model of Working Lungs

You will need 2 balloons, 2 rubber bands, an empty clear plastic soda bottle with the label taken off (a 20-ounce soda bottle will work), a straw, a small amount of clay, and an X-Acto knife with a grownup to use it.

1. Ask your grownup helper to cut a hole in the bottom of the bottle about the size of a silver dollar with the X-Acto knife.
2. Tie 1 balloon closed (no need to have air in it). Then cut a small part off the bottom of the balloon and stretch it over the bottom of the bottle. Keep it in place with a rubber band.
3. Attach the other balloon to one end of the straw. Keep it in place with a rubber band.
4. Stick the straw (with the balloon attached) into the bottle so that the open end of the straw sticks out. Have the balloon sit about midway down the bottle. (Don't let it sit on the bottom of the bottle.)
5. Keep the straw in place in the mouth of the bottle with the clay. Make sure the whole opening of the bottle around the straw is all sealed with clay.
6. Pull down on the knotted balloon at the bottom. This makes the space inside the bottle get bigger. Notice how this makes the balloon inside the bottle get bigger, too. This shows you how when your lungs expand, they draw air into them, like the balloon. This is how inhaling works. Pretty cool, huh?

Gesundheit!

There are many things you do that may affect your regular breathing rhythm, like coughing, sneezing, crying, laughing, hiccupping, and yawning. Each of these actions is doing different things.

♦ When you cough, you take a deep breath and force a sudden blast of air out of your lungs and out your mouth. This is usually done when something is bothering the lining somewhere in your respiratory tract.

♦ When you sneeze, you are also taking a deep breath and forcing a sudden blast of air out of your lungs, but instead of just coming out your mouth, it launches out of your nose, too. Most of the time, you do this automatically, without you even thinking about it.

♦ When you cry, you take sudden sharp breaths in, followed by many short breaths out. This happens when you have some emotional stimulus.

♦ When you laugh, you are doing much the same as crying, as far as breathing goes. This also happens when you have some emotional stimulus.

♦ When you hiccup, you take sudden, sharp, sometimes painful breaths in. This happens when your diaphragm muscle goes into a spasm and can repeat for several minutes.

♦ When you yawn, you take in a very deep breath with your jaw wide open.

Smoking and Lung Cancer
A not-so-fun fact is that ⅓ of all cancer deaths in the United States are from lung cancer. About 90 percent of people who get lung cancer are smokers.

Breathing Troubles

There are many things that can affect your breathing health. Because getting oxygen to your cells is so important, it's a good idea to take good care of your lungs, for a lifetime of healthy breathing. Most respiratory problems are the result of things that happen outside of your body, like smoking, pollution, infections from viruses or bacteria, or inhaling food by mistake.

Get Out of Here

Your body has an amazing ability to get rid of the things that are bothering it. These powerful reactions help remove the dirt and gunk that might be blocking an important airway.

Count the dots to find in each get-out-of-here-now body reaction. Then, multiply the number of dots in each puzzle as directed to find out exactly how fast your body can get rid of the gunk!

# of dots _____ x 5 = _____ miles per hour

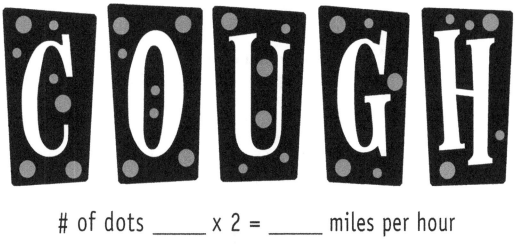

# of dots _____ x 2 = _____ miles per hour

WORDS TO KNOW

allergy

When your body is irritated by something, it can become very sensitive to it and react to it. This is called an allergic reaction. People with allergies have to be careful to avoid the things that they are allergic to or their body will react to them.

People who smoke their whole lives often develop the disease *emphysema* when they get older. This is when the little alveoli in their lungs break down, so there is less area for gas exchange. Someone with emphysema can breathe just as much as anyone, but will still feel starved for oxygen. There is no cure for emphysema, so it's best to avoid getting it in the first place.

Smokers can also get lung cancer. A person gets lung cancer when inhaled smoke from cigarettes over time bothers the regular lung cells so much that they begin to change and grow wildly. The bad cells then continue to spread and soon they take over the lungs and the patient often dies.

When You Can't Breathe . . . Nothing Else Matters

People, and often children, who are exposed to pollution or secondhand smoke or have a lot of allergies can get asthma. This is when your airways get bothered or irritated and the small muscles that surround the bronchi squeeze down tight, not letting enough air get through. It feels a bit like trying to breathe through a straw. It can be very scary. There are medicines that can make the bronchiole muscles relax and open up the airways. It is best to avoid smoke and protect your lungs for life.

Rocky Mountain High

Visiting a place at high altitude, like a ski trip to the mountains, can affect your breathing. At higher altitudes there is less oxygen in the air. You have to breathe more to get the amount of oxygen your body needs. Over a few days your body will get used to the thinner air. One of the ways it does this is by making more red blood cells to carry oxygen. If you try to exercise too soon when visiting the high mountains, your body can react with headaches, panting, dehydration, and even a heart attack. Take your time up high!

FUN FACTS

No Lazy Sharks

Most sharks don't have the muscles that fish have for pumping water into their mouths. They must swim all the time to keep the water, with its oxygen, flowing into their bodies and over their gills. If they stop swimming, they will actually drown!

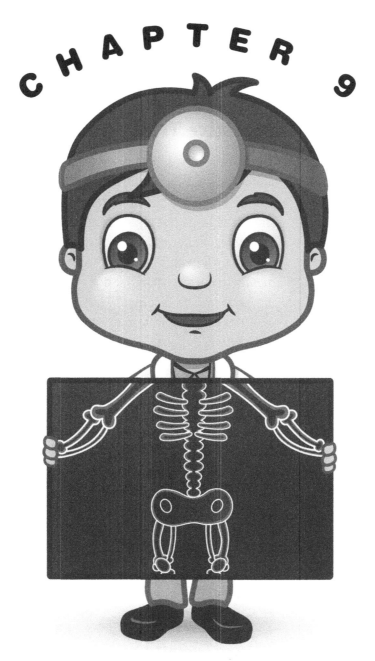

## CHAPTER 9

I'M HUNGRY! THE DIGESTIVE SYSTEM

The Long and Winding Road—Your Digestive Tract

The food you eat has to go on a long journey, passing through many organs in your body. This is called your *digestive tract* (or alimentary canal). It includes your mouth, esophagus, stomach, and small and large intestines. Your digestive tract is mostly a long, hollow, muscular tube. Sometimes it goes straight, but often it is all coiled up. It is open to the outside world at both ends. This means that even though it doesn't look like it, the inside of your digestive system is actually open to the outside of your body!

The digestive system gives you the energy you need to get through life. It does this by doing several important tasks.

◆ It takes in food.
◆ It breaks the food down.
◆ It takes the broken-down food into the blood, where it gets delivered to hungry cells.
◆ It gets rid of the parts of the food that are indigestible as waste.

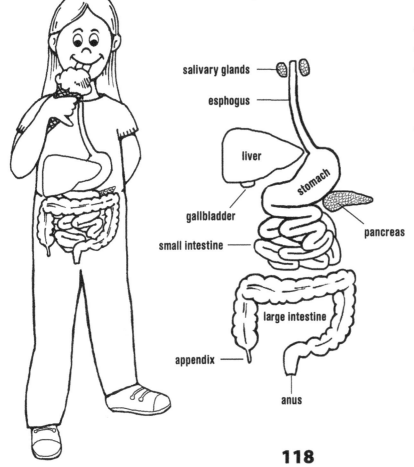

salivary glands

esphogus

liver

stomach

gallbladder

pancreas

small intestine

large intestine

appendix

anus

A Little Help from Your Friends

Your digestive tract gets help breaking down food from other organs like your teeth, tongue, salivary glands, liver, gallbladder, and pancreas. These are also known as your accessory digestive organs. Food is broken down mechanically by chewing and churning, and chemically by digestive juices. Some of the mechanical and chemical digestion is done by the organs of the digestive tract and some is done by the accessory digestive organs. Together they get the job done.

Chew Your Food—Digestion Begins in Your Mouth

Even before you eat food, when you smell, see, or even just think about food, your mouth can water. This is the beginning of digestion. When you put food in your mouth, a lot of things happen. First, you taste it. This helps you decide if you like it. Your mouth is a food-processing machine made of muscle, bone, teeth, and glands. Here are some of the things that happen to the food in your mouth.

- Powerful, muscular lips and cheeks keep the food in your mouth and between your teeth.
- Your teeth grind and tear food down into smaller bits that are easier to digest.
- Your bony palette, which forms the roof of your mouth, is a hard surface against which your tongue can press and turn food during chewing.
- Salivary glands squirt saliva into your mouth to mix with the food. Saliva contains proteins called *enzymes* that start breaking down some foods and help squish it all into a soft mass of food called a *bolus*. This makes it easy to swallow.

WORDS TO KNOW

bolus
The small, round, soft mass of chewed food that you swallow is called a bolus of food.

Health Tip

KEEP A HEALTHY SMILE!

Your teeth are an important part of digestion, and they also help you enjoy your food. Chewing food releases the flavors that you love. Healthy teeth are also attractive and add to your good looks. It's important to take good care of your teeth so you have them your whole life. Make sure that you brush your teeth after eating, at least twice a day. Also try to floss between your teeth every night before you go to bed.

Bad Breath

Bad breath, also called *halitosis*, can come from not brushing your teeth, but it can also happen if the salivary glands are not putting out enough saliva to clean out your mouth regularly throughout the day.

WORDS TO KNOW

amylase

Amylase is a helpful substance (enzyme) in the saliva that breaks down starchy foods into simple sugars to be used by the body.

◆ Your tongue is another powerful muscle that grabs food and keeps it pushed between your teeth for chewing. It also helps mix the food with saliva.

◆ When the food is chewed, wet, and squished into a little bolus, you swallow and your muscular throat (pharynx) contracts and pulls food down into the esophagus.

◆ From here, food travels down your esophagus toward your stomach. The journey through your esophagus can be up to 10 inches long.

Mouthwatering Foods—The Salivary Glands

There are several salivary glands that squirt out saliva when you eat. They are under your tongue, in each cheek, and behind your chin. They squirt saliva into your mouth through little tubes called ducts. Saliva has many jobs:

◆ It helps clean the mouth after you eat.

◆ It breaks up food chemicals so that you can taste your food better.

◆ It wets food so it can be formed into a bolus for swallowing.

◆ The enzymes in saliva start the chemical breakdown of starchy foods.

What Is Spit?

Saliva is mostly water, but it has a strong enzyme in it, called *salivary amylase*. Salivary amylase begins digesting starch in your mouth. A piece of starchy bread in your mouth is broken down by chewing but also begins to be digested. Peanuts or meat, which are made of protein, on the other hand, are just chewed smaller and don't begin to be digested until they reach the stomach.

Saliva also has some chemicals that will help kill off bacteria, viruses, or fungi that are in your food and will slow down bacteria that might grow in your mouth and rot your teeth.

"Borborygmus"

This is a very old word that describes a common sound that your digestive system makes. Follow the directions to learn what it is!

Change the **B** to **ST** _____

Change the first **R** to an **M** _____

Change the **Y** to **ROWL** _____

Move the **G** to the middle _____

Change **MUS** to **ING** _____

Change **BOR** to **ACH** _____

Your Rumbling Tummy—The Stomach

The food you eat travels through your long digestive tract, but it spends more time in your stomach than in any other part of your digestive system. The stomach is about 10 inches long and starts where the esophagus dumps food into it at one end and ends where it funnels the digested food into the small intestine at the other side. Like a balloon, your stomach is small when empty but can stretch a lot bigger when you fill it up. Empty, it is only about the size of a pint, like the milk carton you can get at school. If you keep eating, however, you can stretch it to the size of a gallon of milk!

The stomach's job is to continue breaking down food. It does this in many ways, while also protecting itself from the harsh job of digestion. Here are some of the things your stomach does:

◆ The stomach uses its muscular walls to squeeze, stir, pound, and mush your food down to smaller and smaller bits. It also

FUN FACTS

A Pit of Acid

The acid released in your stomach for digestion is so harsh and dangerous that the walls of your stomach have to be coated with a thick mucus or they would get digested along with your food! The environment in your stomach is 100,000 times more acidic than your blood.

Health Tip

ABOUT THROWING UP...

Throwing up is no fun at all, but there is usually a reason for it. It can happen if you have eaten something with bad bacteria in it, too many spices, or even just too much food. It can happen if you have a virus or have an allergic reaction to a food or medicine. You can even throw up if you see or smell something that you don't like. When the body wants to throw up, or vomit, there is usually nothing you can do to stop it. The order often comes right from your brain. So you might as well get it over with, and then rinse your mouth with water and brush your teeth. Those stomach acids are not good for your teeth! After you are feeling better, drink some water to make up for fluids you lost.

stirs the stomach's digestive juices into the food to help get digestion going.

- The stomach releases another enzyme called *pepsin* for digesting proteins in your food—things like nuts, eggs, and meat.
- Special cells in the stomach lining release a strong acid— hydrochloric acid—to kill off any bacteria you ate with your food. It also helps to start protein digestion.
- Your stomach also makes and releases a thick mucus to line its walls and protect it from its own acids.
- Though most food nutrients are taken into the blood in the intestines, the stomach absorbs many medicines, including aspirin. It also takes in alcohol.

Vitamin B Is Life or Death

The stomach does one more thing that you should know about, and it might be the most important thing of all. It makes and releases a chemical called *intrinsic factor*. Intrinsic factor allows the intestines to take vitamin B_{12} from the foods you eat. Vitamin B_{12} is not found in plants, so if you are a vegetarian, you need to take your vitamins. Vitamin B_{12} is important because you need it to make red blood cells. Without red blood cells, your body can't pick up and deliver oxygen. Without oxygen everything stops, including your life!

Leaving Your Stomach Behind

By the time food leaves your stomach, it has been digested down to a creamy paste called *chyme*. Your stomach will empty almost completely about 4 hours after your meal. All the food will then have passed into your small intestine. When the food finally leaves your stomach, the stomach folds in on itself like an accordion and stays quite small until you eat again.

Fooling Your Stomach

You can trick your stomach into working before you eat a thing. Sometimes the stomach reacts to foods before you eat them by starting to make stomach juices. You can get it to do this by seeing, smelling, tasting, or even thinking about food.

1. Choose a night your family is making a meal that you love.
2. Skip afternoon snacks so that you will be hungry at dinner-time.
3. Right before dinner, go to the stove and look at the food. Smell the food. Think about how good it will taste. Think about how good it will feel to chew it and swallow it. Put a small amount of the food on a spoon and just take one lick so you can taste it, but don't eat it. Do you feel your mouth watering?
4. How does your stomach feel? Is it moving? Is it making any noises? Are you hungrier now than you were before this experiment started? You have tricked your stomach into going to work early!

Health Tip

BURNING, CHURNING MESS

Sometimes a person's stomach stops making the thick mucus it needs to protect it from being burned by its own acids. This can happen when a person is under a lot of stress or drinks too much coffee or alcohol. The stomach lining will start to be eaten away. This is called an ulcer and it hurts!

Where Food Really Feeds You— The Small Intestine

The small intestine comes right after your stomach in the digestive tract. It is a hollow, muscular tube, but it is twisted and turned on itself in a small area in your belly. It is only about an inch wide, but it is the longest part of the digestive tract, running about 6 feet long. If you could relax all the muscles of the small intestine you could actually stretch it out to about 20 feet long!

Ooey Gooey

Mucus is a gooey substance oozed out by the lining of your nose, your lungs, and your digestive tract. It's mostly made of water and salts, but a protein called "mucin" gives it a nice squishy texture. You should be very glad that your stomach has a thick lining of mucus. Why? Put the words from the stomach in order to find out! Use the space at the bottom of the page.

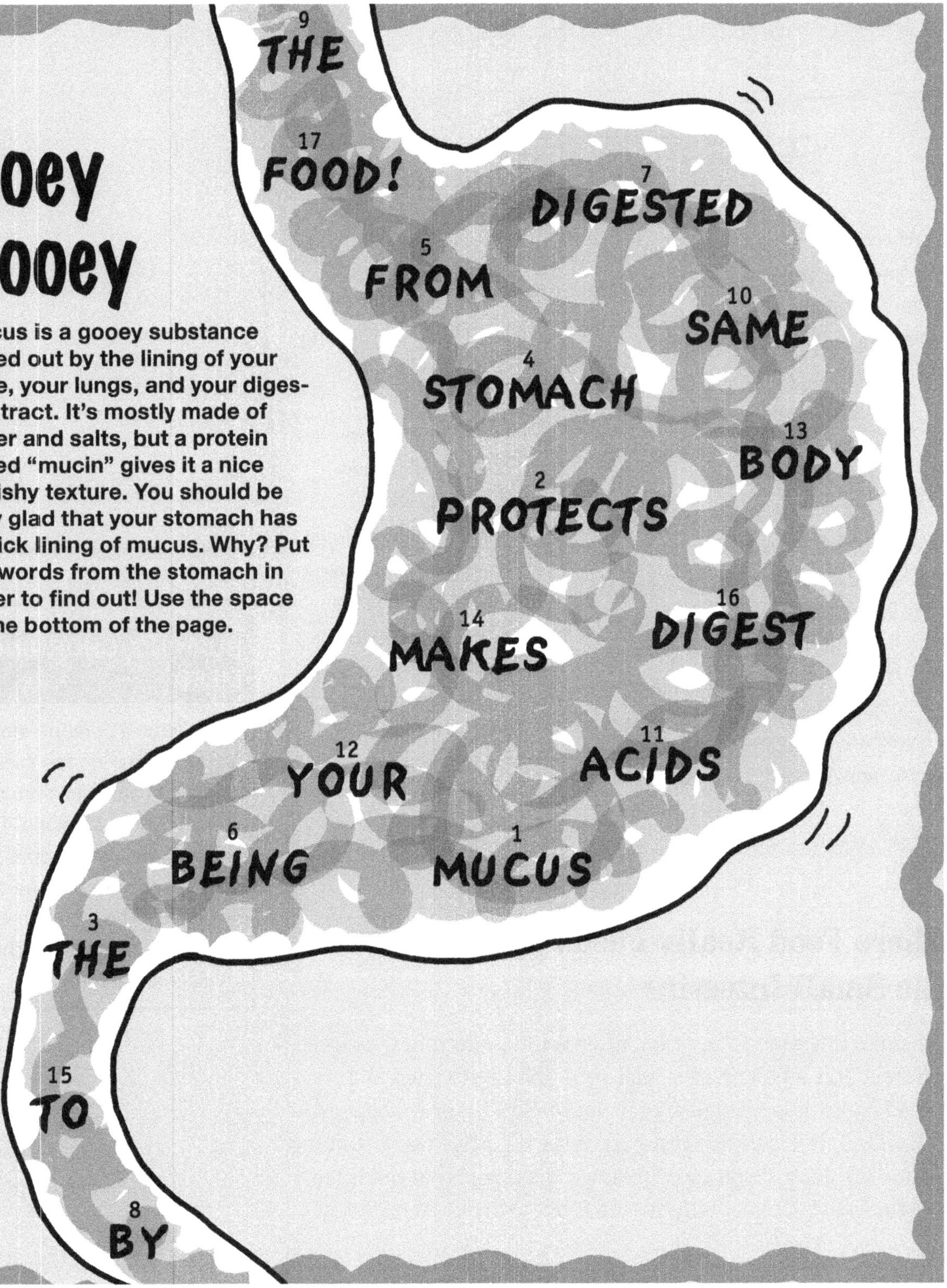

9 THE

17 FOOD!

7 DIGESTED

5 FROM

10 SAME

4 STOMACH

13 BODY

2 PROTECTS

16 DIGEST

14 MAKES

12 YOUR

11 ACIDS

6 BEING

1 MUCUS

3 THE

15 TO

8 BY

The inside of the small intestine takes in the nutrients from the foods you eat. There are 3 things that make the lining of the small intestine good at bringing nutrients into your bloodstream. All of them make the inside of the small intestine bigger and better able to suck in more food (absorb food nutrients).

1. The small intestine has folds, like the stomach, that spread out like an accordion when it is full of food to make the inside bigger. This makes more area that can absorb food nutrients.
2. The walls of the small intestine are covered with finger-like villi. This also makes more surface area that can absorb more food nutrients than if it were just flat.
3. Each of the finger-like villi is also covered with even tinier micro-villi (micro means really, really tiny—so tiny that you would need a microscope to see it). This makes even more area that can absorb food nutrients!

By the time food reaches your small intestine, a lot of it is finally broken down enough to be used by the body. It is more of a liquid by this time, though fat digestion is still going on. In the 3-6-hour journey that the food takes to travel through your small intestine, all of the nutrients will be taken (absorbed) into your bloodstream to be used by the rest of the body.

Don't Waste Water! The Job of the Large Intestine

The large intestine travels up, over, and down around the small intestine. The 3 regions of the large intestine are named for this journey—the ascending colon (going up), the transverse colon (going across), and the descending colon (coming back down). However, the large intestine is really made up of several parts; the cecum, appendix, colon, rectum, and anal canal.

Health Tip

THAT ANGRY APPENDIX

The appendix is a pocket in the large intestine that has no job of which we know. Instead it sits collecting bacteria until one day it may just get inflamed and begin to hurt. This is called *appendicitis* and actually hurts a lot. The pain is in the lower right corner of the tummy, so doctors usually know what it is pretty quickly. They will operate to take it out. Sometimes the appendix can burst, and doctors need to operate right away. Not everyone gets appendicitis. It is most common in teenagers, but can happen at any age.

Health Tip

EAT FIBER FOR A SMOOTH MOVE

Fiber in your diet can include whole grains, oats, beans, and vegetables. They make bulk in the large intestine, which helps it do its job by increasing muscle contractions. More bulk also means that your intestines don't have to squeeze down so hard to push the waste (or stool) out of the body. Bulk also softens the stool so it is easier to pass. So eat your fiber for a smooth move!

When You Gotta Go . . .

Food wastes spend from 12–24 hours in the large intestine. The job of the large intestine is to reclaim any water and salts left in the food waste for the body. Its next job is to push the waste along toward the rectum and out of the body. This part often happens right after a meal. The food in your stomach will signal the large intestine to push out the waste it is carrying because more is on the way! That is when you feel the urge to go to the bathroom and move your bowels.

What a Waste!

When everything worth saving has been absorbed from your food it is time to get rid of the rest, now called feces. When you feel the urge to move your bowels you are feeling the defecation reflex. The feces are pushed through your rectum and expelled from your body through your anus. The process of food digestion is complete.

Why You Fart

Having some bacteria in the large intestine is normal and useful to the body. They ferment some of the indigestible things you eat and make vitamins B and K, which you need. However, the bacteria at work also make gas, like methane—up to 500 ml a day! The gas has to go somewhere, so it comes out of your anus, sometimes at the most embarrassing moments. To make matters worse, these gases can have a rather foul odor. You should know, however, that every human on Earth is making gas, too. So you are not the only one passing gas out there—everyone is!

The Organs That Help—The Liver and Gallbladder

The liver is a big organ, made up of 4 lobes and weighing about 3 pounds. It sits right under your diaphragm on your right side, protected by your ribcage. Your liver is one of the most important organs you have, but only a small part of what it does has to do with digestion. That job is making *bile*. Bile is a green, slimy liquid that helps break up the fats you eat when they reach your small intestine. The liver is connected to the small intestine by a tube called the bile duct. The word duct means tube. Bile also helps the small intestine absorb the fats into the bloodstream for the body to use.

The bile is stored in the gallbladder, a small green sac that sits under the liver and is also connected to the bile duct. In the gallbladder the bile gets thicker and stronger. When you eat a fatty meal, it releases some bile into the small intestine through the bile duct to do its work. Fat digestion doesn't even start until it reaches the small intestine. Bile has its work cut out for it every time you eat.

Keeping the Acid Balance

The pancreas is another important organ that helps with digestion. It is an organ and also a gland that makes and releases pancreatic juice into the small intestine through the bile duct. Pancreatic juice has enzymes that break down all kinds of foods. It also helps balance out the acids released from the stomach with your food. The pancreas is your own built-in antacid maker. The pancreas, as mentioned earlier in the endocrine system, also releases the hormone insulin. This is important for getting the sugars in the blood into the cells that need them.

WORDS TO KNOW

defecation (and feces)

The process of expelling waste from your body is called defecation. The waste is called feces or stool. People use many names for feces but they all mean the same thing!

Health Tip

YOU'VE GOT A LOT OF GALL

Sometimes when a person has a very fatty diet, it is too much for the gallbladder to handle. Then the fat and salts in the bile may form hard little crystal pellets called gallstones. These can cause terrible pain and if the doctors can't dissolve them, they may have to operate and take out the gallbladder altogether. If other people in your family have had gallstones, you might need to watch your diet because you might get them, too. A good balance of foods with not too many fats makes a healthier diet for your body.

Tummy Troubles

For every part of your digestive tract there are possible things that can go wrong, for example ulcers, appendicitis, gallstones, diabetes, vomiting, and even bad breath! In most cases you can stay healthy with a good, balanced diet that includes lots of fruits and vegetables, whole grains, lean meats, and small amounts of dairy and fats. It also helps your digestive tract for you to exercise, keep your weight down, and even brush and floss your teeth!

Diarrhea

Watery stool comes from food wastes rushing through the large intestine before it can reabsorb all the water your body needs. This can happen when you have bacteria that bother the large intestine. If a person has diarrhea for too long, like with more serious bacterial infections like dysentery, the person can get dehydrated and in some severe cases die. Usually diarrhea passes after a few hours and you can make up the fluid loss by drinking some water, juice, or sports drink.

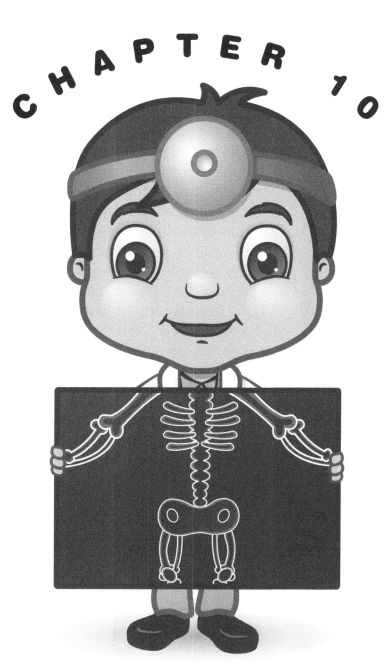

THE DORMANT SYSTEM— REPRODUCTION

Waking Up the Reproductive System

The organ systems you have read about so far work all the time to keep things in your body in balance and running well. From the moment you are born until you die, these body systems run the show. The reproductive system, on the other hand, doesn't even wake up until you reach puberty.

The organs of the reproductive system are different for boys than they are for girls, but their purpose is the same—to make new children. These organs include a pair of primary sex organs and their accessory sex organs (the other organs that help out). The accessory sex organs include glands, ducts, and the sex organs on the outside of the body (also called the external genitalia or genitals).

Boys' Bodies

In boys, the main sex organs are the two testes (or testicles). The testes make sperm. They are also endocrine glands and make the hormone testosterone. All the other sex organs, including the other glands, ducts, and the penis, are accessory sex organs and just help out. They help protect the sperm and get it to the egg for fertilization.

Where Sperm Live

The testes are protected by 2 fibrous layers, plus a tough outer sac, called the *scrotum*. Inside, the testes are made up of long, coiled tubules where the sperm are made. Once a boy passes through puberty, his testes will make sperm for the rest of his life. When the sperm are needed, they will travel down the long tubule inside the testes and out through the penis, to the outside world. This is the same passageway used for urination, but urine

130

Male Reproductive Tract

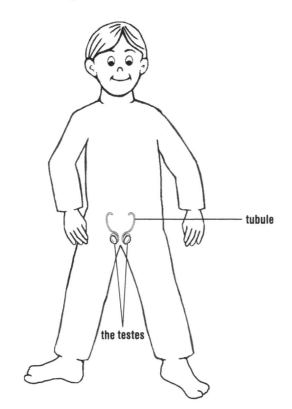

tubule

the testes

FUN FACTS

Why do the testes hang outside the body where they can be hurt?
Men have asked this question from the beginning of time. Only with modern science have we discovered the reason. It is because at 98°F, the inside of the human body is too warm for sperm production. Sperm are made at 93°F, so the testes must hang away from the warm body to make sperm.

comes from the bladder and not the testes. Urine also passes this way several times a day, while the sperm spend most of their time stored inside the testes.

Swimming Sperm

Because sperm travel by swimming, they actually have a tail that beats, moving them forward. They have to be in a liquid to swim, so as they pass down the tubule toward the penis, several glands release fluid into the tubule to help the sperm on their way. The sperm together with the fluid from the accessory sex glands are called *semen*.

FUN FACTS

Race for Life
Only 1 sperm will fertilize the egg, so when the sperm race toward the egg it is a race for their lives! Sperm are only fast if you consider their tiny size—smaller than the eye can see. In reality, they can only travel about 9 inches an hour.

A Lot of Sperm

Every time a man releases sperm it is called an ejaculation. Each ejaculation releases up to 500 million sperm! Only 1 of those sperm will fertilize the egg.

What Is a Sperm Really?

You might know that it takes sperm to fertilize an egg to make a baby grow, but what is sperm really? Sperm contains a set of the genetic code from the father for the future baby, just as the egg contains that information from the mother. So the sperm provides just half of the information needed to make a new person.

The Real King

Many people think that the penis is the main sex organ in a man. This might be because it is the one located outside the body that can be seen. In truth, the testes are the main sex organ. The penis is just the delivery system, like your garden hose delivering water to the lawn.

Pimples Popping Up

When boys and girls go through puberty, their skin and hair get oilier. This is because the oil glands in the skin are woken up with the reproductive system. One side effect of this is pimples. Though some teenagers get worse pimples than others, almost everyone gets at least some. This can be an embarrassing time for boys and girls, but you should know that everyone goes through it!

Puberty in Boys

When a boy goes through puberty at about 14 years old, the testes begin to release the hormone testosterone. Testosterone wakes up the reproductive system and many things begin to happen:

- The body, including the face, gets hairy.
- The boy may get a lot taller suddenly.
- His muscles will get bigger.
- His voice will get lower and deeper.
- He may begin to notice girls in a way he never has before.
- He may get pimples.
- The testes will begin to make sperm.
- The penis will grow longer.

When puberty is complete, a boy has reached his adult form. He is a man.

Super Sized

Who is the biggest person that you know of? Is it your dad? A famous football player? Or maybe a professional wrestling champ! It is hard to imagine that these tall, muscular (or maybe even fat) people were at one time exactly the same size as you and me. How is this possible? Use the decoder to help solve this puzzle.

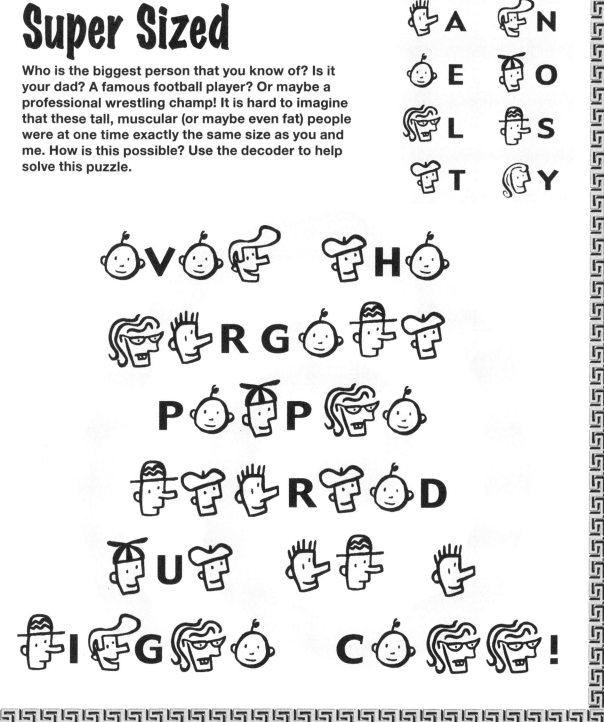

Girls' Bodies

In girls, the main sex organs are the ovaries. The 2 ovaries release the eggs. They are also endocrine glands that make the hormones estrogen and progesterone. All the other sex organs, including the uterus, the uterine tubes (which bring the egg to the uterus), and the vagina are accessory sex organs that help get the sperm and egg together to grow a baby.

The ovaries are about the size of an almond and sit on either side of the uterus in the belly. A girl is born with all the eggs she will ever have in her 2 ovaries. She does not make any more eggs in her lifetime, the way a boy makes sperm throughout his life.

Female Reproductive Tract

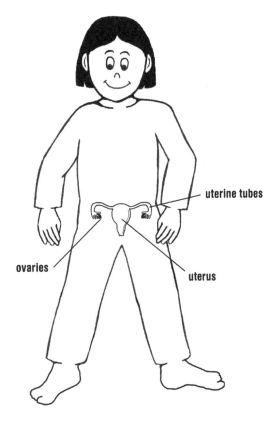

uterine tubes

ovaries

uterus

Puberty in Girls

When a girl reaches puberty at between 10–15 years old, the ovaries will begin to release the hormones estrogen and progesterone. These hormones will wake up the reproductive system and many things begin to happen:

◆ She will start to release an egg every month from her ovaries.
◆ She will start growing taller and her breasts will get bigger.
◆ She will grow hair under her arms and in her pubic area.
◆ She may begin to notice boys in a way she never has before.
◆ She may get pimples.
◆ She may get heavier around her hips and bottom.
◆ She will begin her menstrual cycles.

When puberty is complete, a girl has reached her adult form. She is a woman.

Releasing Eggs

When an egg is released from the ovaries every month, it is called *ovulation*. The egg will travel down the tube into the uterus. The uterus prepares itself for getting a fertilized egg every month. If the egg is fertilized by a sperm, it will happen in the uterine tube before it reaches the uterus. Then it will implant in the wall of the uterus and begin to develop into a baby.

A girl's reproductive system is much more complicated than a boy's because her body will hold and care for a growing baby if 1 of her eggs is fertilized.

If the egg is not fertilized, the uterus wall will begin to break down and another menstrual cycle will begin.

The Menstrual Cycle

Every 28 days a woman goes through a complete menstrual cycle. There are several phases of the menstrual cycle. This is roughly how they work (though they can be slightly different for every woman): Every month a woman's ovaries spend about 10 days getting ready to release an egg. When an egg is released, it is called ovulation. At ovulation the egg travels down the uterine tube to the uterus. There are up to 3 days when this egg can be fertilized before it reaches the uterus. If it is not fertilized, in 14 days the menses will begin—the woman will get her period. This marks the end of 1 menstrual cycle. Then it will start all over again.

Pregnancy and the Body

You now know about sperm and eggs and how they have to get together to result in fertilization and to make a baby grow. The time between fertilization and the birth of the baby is the pregnancy or gestation period.

After everything you have learned about the human body, it is amazing to think that we each grow from a single cell. No

WORDS TO KNOW

zygote
A zygote forms when a sperm binds with an egg at fertilization. This is the first cell of a growing embryo.

embryo
From 3 weeks after fertilization to about 8 weeks, the growing fetus is called an embryo.

fetus
From 9 weeks after fertilization until it's born, the growing baby is called a fetus.

WORDS TO KNOW

placenta
An organ that only develops during pregnancy, the placenta provides food, oxygen, hormones, and waste disposal for the growing baby. Once the baby is born, the placenta is passed out of the mother and thrown away.

wonder people call it the miracle of birth. The development of a new human being really is a remarkable thing.

That first whole cell that results from a sperm and egg getting together at fertilization, each contributing its half of its genetic code, is called a *zygote*. The zygote grows over the next few weeks into an embryo. Then after a couple of months it grows into a fetus. After 280 days and birth this cell will be an infant!

Feeding the Baby

For the 9 months after fertilization, this cell lives and grows inside the uterus of a woman. Many things happen during that time. While it grows and develops, it gets all its oxygen and food from its mother through the placenta. The placenta is an organ that only develops during pregnancy. Through the placenta, a developing baby gets a little bit of anything the woman takes into her body. This includes oxygen, food, and even medicine. This is why pregnant women have to be very careful. Alcohol, drugs, and even illnesses, like measles, during pregnancy can get through her bloodstream and affect the growing baby.

Growing a New Person

During the 9 months of pregnancy, the woman's body is changing, too. For the first 3 months she may experience a queasy feeling, especially in the morning. This is referred to as morning sickness and is common among pregnant women.

Over the next few months, the fetus will be growing and taking up a lot more room that used to be where all her organs lived. At night, when the woman is lying down, the baby can press down on her stomach, bladder, and intestines and make her uncomfortable. She may have to urinate more often. Some foods won't taste good and she may not be able to eat much at one time. Her breasts will grow in preparation for feeding the baby.

By the end of the pregnancy, her feet may be swollen and she may be pretty tired. It's hard work to grow a new person!

It's a Baby!

After 9 months, the baby is fully developed and ready to be born. Though the woman may be ready to be done carrying the baby, the hardest part is still to come. She must deliver the baby. This is called labor and delivery, and if you ask any woman who has had a baby, she will tell you that it is a lot of work! A woman's first birth can take at least 14 hours of labor before the baby is ready to be delivered.

When the baby is born, it takes its first breath and its lungs open up and start to work. The placenta, which was attached to

That's a Big Baby!
Human babies weigh from 5–10 pounds at birth. A newborn blue whale weighs more than 100 pounds. A baby elephant can weigh 250 pounds at birth!

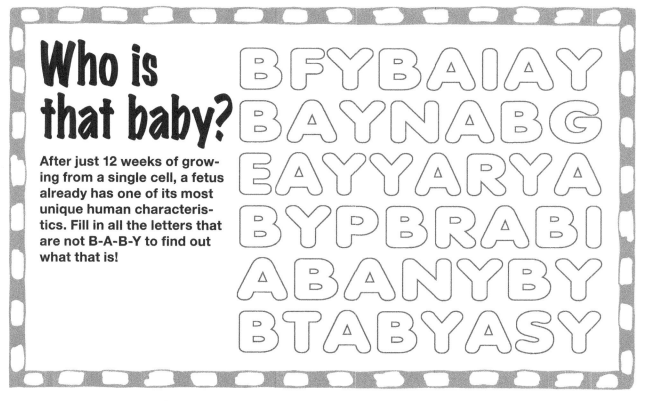

Who is that baby?

After just 12 weeks of growing from a single cell, a fetus already has one of its most unique human characteristics. Fill in all the letters that are not B-A-B-Y to find out what that is!

The Large and Small of It
According to the *Guinness Book of World Records*, the heaviest human baby ever born was in Canada and weighed almost 24 pounds! The smallest surviving human baby was born in the United Kingdom and weighed just 10 ounces.

the baby through the belly button, can then be separated from the baby. Now that it is separate from its mother, the baby will get hungry! The mother's breasts, stimulated by hormones, start to make milk, and soon after the birth she can begin to feed her new baby.

Name That Baby

A baby human is called an infant. A baby tiger is called a cub. Can you name the babies of these animals?

A baby horse is a _____

A baby seal is a _____

A baby fox is a _____

A baby bear is a _____

A baby kangaroo is a _____

A baby bison is a _____

A baby bird is a _____

A baby llama is a _____

Can you think of any more?

Answers: colt, pup, kit, cub, joey, calf, chick, cria

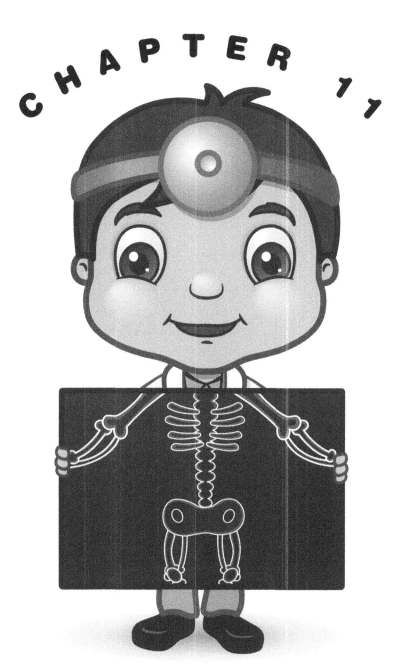

CHAPTER 11

AN OWNER'S MANUAL FOR YOUR BODY

Aging and Your Body

No matter what else happens to you in your lifetime, one thing will happen for sure—you will age. Aging is a natural part of life, though people fight against it the best they can. With age you can expect many things to happen to your body, for instance:

- As you age, your skin will stop replacing the surface cells as quickly after they are rubbed off, so your skin will get thinner and bruise more easily. The oil glands will slow down, so your skin will get drier and feel less soft. You will get wrinkles. You can slow this process down a lot by taking care of your skin now, while you are young. Stay out of the sun at midday, cover up when you are in the sun, and wear sunscreen. It will make a difference and you will be glad you did it later!
- Your hair follicles decrease, so your hair will thin. It will also turn gray, though when that happens varies for different people.
- Your muscles will lose strength and size with age. This doesn't just affect your physical fitness. Remember that your muscles are responsible for your breathing, bladder control, and other body systems. Luckily, you can slow the aging of muscles, too. Exercise is important at all stages of your life to keep your muscles strong, but especially as you get old. Stay active!
- Your bones become more brittle and your joints can break down as you age. Again, exercise has a marked effect on slowing down bone aging.
- Your eyesight will change, usually making you more far-sighted.

It's Not All Bad News!

This may all sound like bad news, but the truth is, older people are healthier and more active than ever before. Aging can bring a lot of satisfaction, too.

You may have a family and even grandchildren to spend time with. You will have a collection of friends and great experiences to remember and continue to build on. Many people travel, visit family, start new hobbies, and do the things they never had time to do while they were younger and busier.

The key is to stay healthy. Read on for a review of the things you need to do to stay healthy and live a good, long life.

Can You Live Forever?

People are living a lot longer than they used to, especially in the United States. This is because we have learned ways to stay healthy and avoid the things that kill us! Here is a list of some of the things we now know about staying healthy and living longer.

- We know the right foods to eat and are able to get healthy foods all year round.
- We know about washing germs off our hands and food to prevent many illnesses. Wash your hands several times a day.
- Children used to die of many dangerous childhood illnesses that are now almost completely gone because we immunize kids against them. These include polio, diphtheria, measles, whooping cough, and tetanus.
- We know about getting regular exercise our whole lives.
- We know that smoking is very bad for you.
- We know that drinking too much alcohol is bad for you. Limit how much you drink, or don't drink at all.
- We can treat many aging diseases like osteoporosis and diabetes.
- We have gotten better at treating all kinds of illnesses and diseases throughout people's lives. Ask your parents and doctor for help if you don't feel well.
- We know that keeping the brain stimulated by reading, learning, and interacting with other people helps it stay aware and working even into old age. Keep learning your whole life.
- We have better care for aged people.

A Longer Life
People today are living longer than their grandparents. According to the Centers for Disease Control, the average American will live for almost 78 years. That is a lot longer than just 100 years ago. The average life span in 1900 was only 47!

Super Body Crossword

ACROSS

4. Your body's largest organ. Hint: It's stretched all over you!

5. Nose explosion.

6. Strap that keeps your body safe in a car accident.

9. Creases in old skin.

12. A bad case of pimples.

15. Small body parts that ooze hormones into your blood.

17. Chemical messenger that travels in the blood.

18. A tiny new person.

19. The building blocks of your body. They form tissues, organs, and you!

22. This grows out of a follicle. It can be straight or curly.

25. Large, round, hollow bone made up of 22 different parts.

26. Where two bones come together.

30. These tubes carry blood away from the heart.

32. Muscle that pumps.

33. A gooey blob of blood.

34. Bumpy little tongue cells.

DOWN

1. The body system that supports you, like beams in a building.

2. Gooey stuff that surrounds an infection. It's full of white blood cells.

3. Three letters that are the blueprint for everything that's you!

5. Main highway for nerves and messages.

7. Another name for your intestines.

8. Do cats make you sneeze and wheeze? You have an _____!

10. A dad's reproductive cell.

11. Hip bones.

13. Important and colorful body fluid.

14. Unique pattern on tips of our digits.

16. You get these from the food you eat. Your body needs them to stay healthy.

20. Air goes in and out of these.

21. Slab of dried blood that covers a cut.

23. These body parts pull and pull.

24. Food's first stop after you swallow.

27. These cells carry electrical messages all over your body.

28. This nutrient is clear and wet.

29. These tubes carry blood to the heart.

31. A mom's reproductive cell.

WORDS TO KNOW

hydrogenated

A chemical process by which hydrogen is added to liquid oils to turn them into semi-solid or solid fats.

partially hydrogenated oil

During food processing, liquid oils are changed to partially hydrogenated oils because they last longer on store shelves without going bad. They have also been found to contribute to heart disease.

Health Tip

SHOP CO-OP

If you have a local food co-op, ask your parents to check it out. They often have very healthy food, including organic fruits, vegetables and grains, pure bulk foods, and treats made with honey and maple syrup.

You Are What You Eat—The Right Food for a Healthy Life

As mentioned earlier, a good, balanced diet helps keep your body growing strong and healthy throughout your life. Research shows that eating the right foods can actually stop some very bad diseases later in life, like heart disease, cancer, and strokes. But more than that, you are still growing. You need to eat right so that:

◆ Your bones can grow straight and strong
◆ Your skin can be clear and healthy
◆ You don't get cavities and have perfect teeth your whole life
◆ You have the fuel you need to learn at school
◆ You stay trim and have energy to work and play

Start eating well when you are a kid. Eating habits can last a lifetime!

Learn to Hate Hydrogenate!

Many of the foods you see at the grocery store are healthy foods that you need to grow and thrive, but some should be avoided. Scientists now know that partially hydrogenated oils are not good for us. Why? Partially hydrogenated oils are made when liquid oils are hydrogenated to preserve them longer. This turns them into trans fats. Trans fats are very bad for you. They clog arteries and add to heart disease. Not good! They are in many of the processed foods we buy at the store, like cookies and crackers. Look for foods that use vegetable oils instead of partially hydrogenated oils.

High Fructose-Free

Another controversial ingredient that is becoming more common in foods is high-fructose corn syrup. It is cheaper than sugar and lasts longer on the shelf, but may have some bad side effects. High-fructose corn syrup is in soft drinks, fruit juices, cookies, and many, many foods you might never expect (like tomato sauce). Many scientists are worried that high-fructose corn syrup is making us fatter and may lead to more obesity and even diabetes. Look for foods that use sugar, honey, or maple syrup instead of high-fructose corn syrup. Or better yet, eat fruit instead of drinking fruit juice!

Use It or Lose It—Getting Active to Stay Healthy

You don't have to be a marathon runner to be healthy and athletic. As a matter of fact, walking, riding your bike, and swimming may be the healthiest exercises there are, and they are fun, too! Here are some other ways to get exercise that might be fun for you:

- Walk the dog
- Wash the car
- Dig in the garden or rake some leaves
- Play Frisbee, softball, basketball, or other sports with friends after school or on the weekend
- Jump on a trampoline or jump rope
- Go horseback riding or just brush down a horse
- Go rollerblading or skateboarding
- Build a snowman
- Play badminton or Ping-Pong

WORDS TO KNOW

high-fructose corn syrup

High-fructose corn syrup is being used as a sweetener in many processed foods rather than sugar because it is cheaper and lasts longer on the shelf without going bad.

FUN FACTS

Get Moving, America!
Even though we know it is good for us, research shows that more than half of all Americans don't get enough regular exercise. We need to get moving!

Health Tip

HOW MUCH EXERCISE IS ENOUGH?

The Department of Health and Human Services (HHS) and the Department of Agriculture (USDA) recommend, in their Dietary Guidelines for Americans, that children and teenagers get at least 60 minutes of exercise every day.

TRY THIS

Family Fun

Most grownups need more exercise than they get. You can help your parents out by getting them to be active with you, too. Ask your mom or dad to play tennis, shoot some baskets, or just go for a walk with you today.

Exercise Journal

Make an exercise journal to plan the activities you want to do every week. Be optimistic about what you can do, but don't overload your schedule so that you burn out or can't complete your goals. Mix up the kind of exercise so it stays fun. If you are running around playing soccer one day, choose an activity to work your upper body the next day, like basketball or tennis. Use an old notebook to plan your week or download a calendar online.

Taking Care of Your Body

By now you have probably gotten the idea that if you eat healthy, low-fat foods and get regular exercise, you can live longer and have a full, thriving life. What other things will keep your body going strong for a long time to come? Here are some quick tips:

- Wash your hands regularly to shed the germs picked up in everyday life before they can get you sick.
- Avoid being out in the sun at the peak of the day, from 11 A.M. to 3 P.M. If you have to be out in the sun, wear sunscreen or cover up with a wide-brimmed hat.
- Always wear a seatbelt when riding in a car.
- Always wear a helmet when riding a bike or downhill skiing.
- Don't smoke cigarettes, and if you are around someone who smokes, move away while that person is smoking.
- Don't blow your ears out listening to music. Hearing loss is permanent.
- Brush your teeth. Losing your teeth can affect what you can eat and is not pretty.

Have fun, but protect your body. It's the only one you get!

GLOSSARY

abdominal
Abdominal describes the part of the body containing the digestive organs and extends from under the ribcage to the pelvis.

allergy
When your body is irritated by something it can become very sensitive to it and react to it. This is called an allergic reaction. People with allergies have to be careful to avoid the things that they are allergic to or their body will react to them.

amylase
Amylase is a helpful substance (enzyme) in the saliva that breaks down starchy foods into simple sugars to be used by the body.

anatomical
Something that relates to the anatomy or body structure is called anatomical.

blood vessels
Blood vessels are a complex web of hollow tubes that move blood around all through the body. They include arteries, veins, and capillaries.

bolus
The small, round mass of chewed food that you swallow is called a bolus of food.

bowels
The intestines are sometimes called the bowels. When food moves all the way through the intestine to be removed as waste, it is called moving your bowels.

carpals
The carpals are 8 small bones that make up the base of each of your hands. They sit where the thick, fleshy part of your palm is.

cervical
Cervical describes things having to do with your neck. The cervical vertebrae are the bones in the neck.

chromosome
Chromosomes are butterfly-shaped structures made up of tightly coiled DNA and proteins, found in the nuclei of our cells.

clot
A clot is a thick mass of blood that has turned from a liquid into more of a soft solid, so it will not flow anymore.

contract
When a muscle becomes shorter and more compact in order to move part of the body, it has contracted.

defecation
The process of expelling waste from your body is called defecation. The waste is called feces or stool.

dendrite
Dendrites are the short branches on nerve cells that receive or pass on nerve signals.

diaphragm
The diaphragm is a dome-shaped layer of muscle that separates the chest from the belly. The lungs sit on top of it and are attached to it. The diaphragm pulls down when you inhale, pulling the lungs down with it. This opens them up like a suction cup, drawing oxygen into the lungs. In this way, the diaphragm helps you with your breathing.

diffusion
Diffusion is the spreading out of a gas until it is uniform everywhere. In other words, the oxygen flows from the blood into the alveoli because there is more oxygen in the blood than in the alveoli. Diffusion seeks to make the amount in both places equal, so it flows across the membrane.

embryo
From 3 weeks after fertilization to about 8 weeks, the growing fetus is called an embryo.

endocrine
Endocrine glands secrete hormones directly into the blood. They are compared to exocrine glands, like sweat glands, that secrete through ducts out onto the skin.

fertilization

When a female egg is made ready by a male's sperm to make new offspring, this is called fertilization. It happens in all animals, and many plants as well.

fetus

From 9 weeks after fertilization until it's born, the growing baby is called a fetus.

fibrinogen

Fibrinogen is a substance in the blood that turns into stringy fibers when your blood clots and helps to form a scab.

gene

A gene is a unit of heredity that you get from 1 of your parents. Each gene describes 1 or more of your body traits—like eye or hair color.

genome

A person's genome is 1 complete set of all his or her genes or genetic material.

hemophilia

Hemophilia is a disease where the blood cannot clot because 1 of the needed clotting factors is missing from the body. Until recently, when scientists were able to make clotting factors in the laboratory, most people with hemophilia did not live a very long life.

heredity

Heredity is the passing on of traits from parents to their children.

high-fructose corn syrup

High-fructose corn syrup is being used as a sweetener in many processed foods rather than sugar because it is cheaper and lasts longer on the shelf without going bad.

homeostasis

Your body adjusting to things happening inside and out is important to keep a healthy balance or homeostasis.

hormone

A hormone is a chemical substance released by special cells into the blood to regulate the actions of other cells.

integration

Integration is when you bring things together to make a larger and more complex whole to solve a problem. In the nervous system, the information or stimulus is brought into the brain so the brain can decide how to react to it.

integument

The integument is the tough outer layer of an animal that surrounds and encloses it.

keratin

Tough, waterproof cells called keratin are made deep in the skin and then pushed out toward the surface to help protect you.

ligament

Ligaments are tough bands of connective tissue that hold together 2 bones and help keep joints stable.

mastication

The act of chewing your food is called mastication.

melanin

The pigment or protective coloring that keeps us safe from the ultraviolet (UV) radiation of the sun is called melanin. It's also what makes freckles!

membrane

A membrane is a thin sheet, like a skin, that surrounds and separates something like a cell to keep it apart from the outside environment.

menstrual cycle

Every 28 days a woman goes through a complete menstrual cycle. Her ovaries spend about 10 days getting ready to release an egg. When an egg is released (ovulation) it travels down the uterine tube to the uterus. There are up to 3 days when this egg can be fertilized before it reaches the uterus. If it is not fertilized, in 14 days the menses will begin—she will get her period. This marks the end of 1 menstrual cycle.

metabolism

All the chemical processes that happen inside your body to keep you alive are considered part of your metabolism.

nutrient

A nutrient is something that is used by the body to help with growth, ongoing needs, and repairs.

organelle
Organelles are the "little organs" of a cell that carry out the many jobs that need to be done in a living thing.

oxygenate
This is simply to supply something with oxygen. When the blood is oxygenated in the lungs, it means that the blood picks up the oxygen when you inhale, and then delivers it to the body.

palsy
A palsy is when some muscles become frozen in place (paralyzed) and sometimes have shaky tremors.

paralysis
When someone has paralysis, the person cannot move or feel that part of his or her body.

partially hydrogenated oil
During food processing, liquid oils are changed to partially hydrogenated oils because they last longer on store shelves without going bad. They have also been found to contribute to heart disease.

peripheral nervous system
The peripheral nervous system includes all the nerves outside the brain and spinal cord. The word peripheral means "located on the edge of things," so this is a good description of all the nerves that come off the brain and spinal cord.

phalanges
The phalanges are the bones in your fingers. There are 14 in each hand—3 per finger and 2 in your thumb.

placenta
An organ that only develops during pregnancy, the placenta provides food, oxygen, hormones, and waste disposal for the growing baby. Once the baby is born, the placenta is passed out of the mother and thrown away.

pus
Pus is a whitish fluid that surrounds an infected injury. It is full of white blood cells doing their work to fight infection.

resonate
Your nose is like a resonating chamber, making your voice fuller and deeper. This means that it allows the sound of your voice to bounce around and vibrate to get bigger.

respiratory membrane
The respiratory membrane is the fused wall of the alveoli and the capillary lying next to it. It is across this membrane that oxygen is traded for carbon dioxide.

stimulus
Something in your environment that stirs you up or pesters you is a stimulus. Your body will respond to a stimulus to protect itself. For example, a bad smell will make you move away!

tarsals
The tarsals are the 7 small bones that make up the heel of each of your feet. The 2 largest ones connect to the tibia of the leg.

tendon
A tendon is a strong cord of fiber that attaches a muscle to a bone.

thoracic
Thoracic describes things having to do with your chest region. The thoracic vertebrae are the bones in the thorax (or chest area) that attach to your ribs.

tubule
Tiny, tiny tubes in the body that deliver a substance from one place to another, tubules are found in the kidneys, testes, etc.

urinate
When you drink a lot of juice or water, you have to go to the bathroom to pass water. Scientists call this water urine, and the process of passing urine is called urination. Your body is getting rid of excess water and other wastes that it doesn't need.

vertebrae
The vertebrae are a group of small, irregular-shaped bones that together make up the backbone.

zygote
A zygote forms when a sperm binds with an egg at fertilization. This is the first cell of a growing embryo.

APPENDIX B
WEB RESOURCES

Owl pellet activity sheets
www.makingtrackschallenge
.com/inquiry-based_detail.
php?reference=73

Electroreception in ocean ani-mals
www.elasmo-research.org/
education/white_shark/
electroreception.htm

To learn more about the endo-crine system online
http://yucky.discovery.com/noflash/
body/pg000133.html

To learn about illnesses through the world
http://youthink.worldbank.org/about

About health and nutrition
www.food.gov.uk/healthiereating/
nutcomms

Centers for Disease Control and Prevention: Obesity in the United States
www.cdc.gov/nccdphp/dnpa/
obesity/trend/maps

Teenage health
www.cdc.gov/HealthyYouth/az/
index.htm

Bone health
www.cdc.gov/nccdphp/dnpa/
nutrition/nutrition_for_everyone/
bonehealth/index.htm

Protecting your skin
www.cdc.gov/cancer/skin

Protecting yourself from carbon monoxide
www.cdc.gov/co/default.htm

About diabetes
www.cdc.gov/diabetes

Diet
www.fruitsandveggiesmatter.gov

Kids about nutrition
www.cdc.gov/nccdphp/dnpa/
nutrition/nutrition_for_everyone/
resources/index.htm - For Kids

United States Department of Agriculture: Games about diet and nutrition
www.fns.usda.gov/eatsmartplay
hard

www.choosemyplate.gov/children-over-five.html

Games about health and diet
http://kidshealth.org/kid

http://members.kaiserpermanente
.org/redirects/landingpages/afd

www.cdc.gov/powerfulbones

www.bam.gov/index.html

APPENDIX C
PUZZLE ANSWERS

HEAD TO TOE ◆ PAGE 13

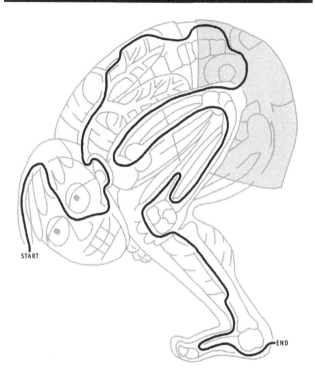

START

END

BUILD A BODY ◆ PAGE 17

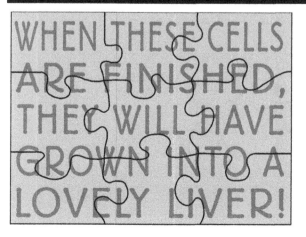

WHEN THESE CELLS ARE FINISHED, THEY WILL HAVE GROWN INTO A LOVELY LIVER!

COPY SHOP ◆ PAGE 20

SKIN ART ◆ PAGE 27

Your thumbprint art might look a little different from ours, but that's OK!

OUT WITH THE OLD ◆ PAGE 32

~~GOLD~~	**YOU**	~~ANTIQUE~~	~~SCOLD~~
~~OUT-DATED~~	~~OLD~~	~~AGED~~	**SHED**
~~COLD~~	**TWO**	~~FOLD~~	**TO**
THREE	~~HOLD~~	**BILLION**	~~ELDERLY~~
~~ANCIENT~~	**CELLS**	~~MOLD~~	~~SOLD~~
EVERY	~~SENIOR~~	**DAY**	~~BOLD~~

BATH TIME ◆ PAGE 35

Q: Why does your skin wrinkle when you stay too long in the bathtub?

A: The outer layer of dead skin cells soak up water. Only parts of it can swell—the rest of it is tightly attached to the skin underneath.

SAY WHAT? ◆ PAGE 41

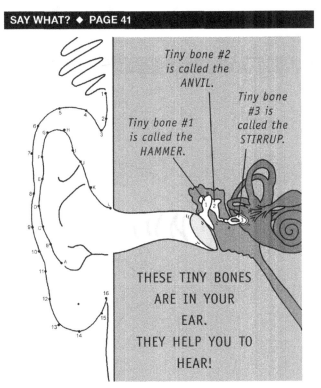

Tiny bone #2 is called the ANVIL.

Tiny bone #3 is called the STIRRUP.

Tiny bone #1 is called the HAMMER.

THESE TINY BONES ARE IN YOUR EAR. THEY HELP YOU TO HEAR!

SHADOW DANCE ◆ PAGE 46

WORD JOINTS ◆ PAGE 49

CAN'T STOP! ◆ PAGE 61

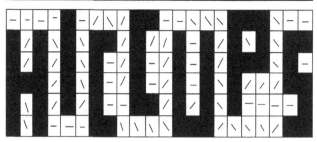

The diaphragm is a large sheet of muscle below the lungs. It helps pull air into the lungs and push it back out again. When the diaphragm starts to spasm and contract uncontrollably, you get hiccups!

PULL AND PULL ◆ PAGE 54

1. HAIRY
2. TALL
3. HEAVY
4. PALE
5. OLD
6. HAPPY

1. BALD
2. SHORT
3. SKINNY
4. DARK
5. YOUNG
6. SAD

YUM OR GROSS ◆ PAGE 67

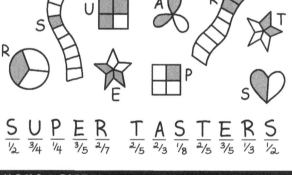

$$S \quad U \quad P \quad E \quad R \quad T \quad A \quad S \quad T \quad E \quad R \quad S$$
$$\tfrac{1}{2} \quad \tfrac{3}{4} \quad \tfrac{1}{4} \quad \tfrac{3}{5} \quad \tfrac{2}{7} \quad \tfrac{2}{5} \quad \tfrac{2}{3} \quad \tfrac{1}{8} \quad \tfrac{2}{5} \quad \tfrac{3}{5} \quad \tfrac{1}{3} \quad \tfrac{1}{2}$$

FROWN OR SMILE? ◆ PAGE 57

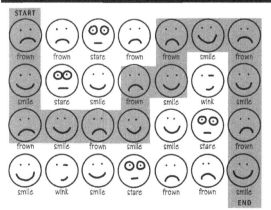

It actually takes about 12 muscles to make either a frown or a smile. Of course, if you are angry and frown really hard (scowl), or if you smile a huge smile (grin), you might use more muscles!

R.U.O.K.? ◆ PAGE 73

THE DOCTOR HITS JUST BELOW THE KNEE AND YOUR LEG KICKS OUT

FACE FARCE ◆ PAGE 75

THERE'S SOMETHING
SMELLY
BETWEEN US!

PERFECT FIT ◆ PAGE 84

CROSSED MESSAGES ◆ PAGE 87

ADDING IODINE ◆ PAGE 89

WHAT'S YOUR TYPE? ◆ PAGE 95

	A	B	AB	O
Sam	✓	✗	✗	✗
Lily		✓		✗
Dan			✓	
Barb			✗	✓

The clues give you information about which blood types the children don't have. These types are marked with an X. The check marks show what blood type each child is.

HIGH TIDE ◆ PAGE 98

THE BLOOD SURGING THROUGH THE VEINS IN YOUR EARS!

CAUTION! ◆ PAGE 109

THEY ARE
THE ONLY
INTERNAL
ORGANS
CONSTANTLY
EXPOSED TO
THE EXTERNAL
ENVIRONMENT!

IN AND OUT ◆ PAGE 112

of your organs that sense smell __1__

# of ears on your body __2__

# of digits on two hands and one foot __15__

# of navels on your body __1__

# of chambers in your heart __4__

YOU BREATHE ABOUT **23** THOUSAND TIMES A DAY!

GET OUT OF HERE ◆ PAGE 115

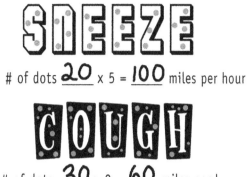

# of dots __20__ x 5 = __100__ miles per hour

# of dots __30__ x 2 = __60__ miles per hour

"BORBORYGMUS" ◆ PAGE 121

STORBORYGMUS

STOMBORYGMUS

STOMBORROWLGMUS

STOMBORGROWLMUS

STOMBORGROWLING

STOMACH GROWLING

OOEY GOOEY ◆ PAGE 124

MUCUS PROTECTS THE STOMACH FROM BEING DIGESTED BY THE SAME ACIDS YOUR BODY MAKES TO DIGEST FOOD!

SUPER SIZED ◆ PAGE 133

EVEN THE LARGEST PEOPLE STARTED OUT AS A SINGLE CELL!

SUPER BODY CROSSWORD ◆ PAGE 142

Across: SKIN, SNEEZE, SEATBELT, WRINKLES, ACNE, GLANDS, HORMONE, BABY, CELLS, HAIR, SKULL, JOINT, ARTERIES, HEART, CLOT, TASTEBUDS

Down: SPINALCORD, PUNGENT, DNA, SEED, TOWEL, ALLERGY, BLOOD, FIBER, PERVIOUS, NUTRIENT, SCRUBBING, STOMACH, MUSCLE, MWATER, VGINGIVON, NERVE

WHO IS THAT BABY? ◆ PAGE 137

FINGERPRINTS

INDEX